D0297734

70000610198 8

OUT OF THE DEPTHS
OF HELL

OUT OF
THE DEPTHS
OF HELL

A Soldier's Story of Life and Death
In Japanese Hands

by

JOHN McEWAN

H.P.L.

LEO COOPER

HARINGEY PUBLIC LIBRARIES	
C.HHV '13	
Morley Books	11.2.00
	£14.95
440.547252	MAC

First published in Great Britain in 1999 by
LEO COOPER
an imprint of
Pen & Sword Books Ltd,
47 Church Street,
Barnsley, South Yorkshire, S70 2AS

ISBN 0 85052 668 X

Copyright © 1999 John McEwan
A CIP record for this book is available from the British Library

Typeset in Bembo by Phoenix Typesetting Ilkley, West Yorkshire.

Printed in England by Mackays of Chatham plc, Chatham, Kent

Dedication

To those of my comrades who slaved and suffered in the vile Formosan copper mine of Kinkasaki and were released by compassionate Death from their lives of brutalized misery at the hands of the Japanese and their fiendish Taiwanese underlings.

Also to my beloved wife, Nan, who so faithfully awaited my return from 'out of the depths' for four long, anxious years and was the light of life that glimmered for me at the end of those grimmest of tunnels – Kinkasaki's claustrophobic caverns.

Contents

Acknowledgements

My thanks to John Dougan, for help in obtaining material from the Imperial War Museum and other sources. I am grateful too to the Trustees of the Imperial War Museum, London, for permission to reproduce the photographs from their archive which appear in this book. Also to Michael Hurst, a member of the Kinkaseki★ Memorial Committee, for the photographs of the Kinkaseki Memorial and the Garden of Remembrance in Chinguashi (as Kinkaseki is now called).

My warmest thanks to Brigadier Henry Wilson, of Pen & Sword Books, for his enthusiasm and kindness, understanding and patience, and for the confidence he has shown in my work from the outset. Also to Brigadier Bryan Watkins, my editor, who at once identified himself with the story and with whom I have worked in friendship to put the finishing touches on the manuscript, as he prepared it for publication. That both 'my Brigadiers' were soldiers and truly understood, was a great advantage.

Finally, I have to thank my dear wife Nan, to whom the book is dedicated, for all her patience, encouragement and help and for suffering the domestic upheaval that the production of any book in a small house cannot fail to create.

J.M.

★ The spelling Kinkasaki for the name of the mine has been used throughout, because that was the name by which all those who worked there knew it, but the correct spelling is as shown here – Kinkaseki.

Kinkasaki: JM and John 'Dempsey' Kane run into trouble with 'Frying Pan'. (JM – *left*)
(*from an original drawing by the Author*)

Out of the Depths

Out of the depths have I cried unto Thee, O Lord, Lord – Lord, hear my voice.

And so it was that, amidst the stifling, searing heat of the 'work holes', with the sweat-streaked grime clinging to my berri-berri ridden skin and bones, I sought to reach the whereabouts of my Creator . . . to let Him or Herself 'up there' see what these foul fiends, the Japanese, had done to me – His, or Her, property. And I prayed, with all my heart and soul, for supervention of my forlorn and melancholy predicament. For time was running out for me . . . fast.

'Tis at times like these that we mortals reach for the proverbial 'straw', when all earthly options have been exhausted in our search for succour, grasping at the hands of our spiritual 'Betters' and praying that they will grasp ours too – with compassionate heavenly reassurance.

Foreword

It was with considerable pride and with bursting self-confidence that I and my fellow Gunners of the 155th (Lanarkshire Yeomanry) Field Regiment Royal Artillery disembarked at Port Swettenham in northern Malaya late in 1941 with our 4.5" howitzers, ready to do battle against whatever enemy might confront us but blissfully unaware that, within weeks, the Japanese would attack Pearl Harbor and subsequently attack northern Malaya. By the time that second attack developed, the Regiment was deployed in readiness and inflicted considerable casualties on the invaders. But, do what we might, there was no way that we were going to stop the floodtide and, fighting as we withdrew, the Regiment soon found itself in Singapore and subsequently a victim of the British surrender. Along with tens of thousands of other troops, we became prisoners of the Japanese and for three and a half years suffered the brutality and torment which that involved.

After some months in the notorious prison camp of Changi in Singapore, a thousand of us were shipped, under appalling conditions, to the island of Taiwan (then called Formosa). There, until the war's end in 1945, we slaved in the terrible copper mine of Kinkasaki.

★ ★ ★

This is the story of that experience. Some names have been substituted in order to avoid causing grief or embarrassment to the families of abused soldiers imprisoned in Changi or at Kinkasaki, or the Jungle Camp of Kukutsu, where life was made hell by our devilish Japanese and Taiwanese guards.

I survived the rigours of that copper mine and the battering of

Corporal Tashi's bloodstained bamboo at Kukutsu because, I am sure, of a merciful intervention by my Maker. My prayers had been answered. It is for those of my unfortunate comrades who did not survive that I forever grieve.

Their torment and tears were also my own and their humiliation mine too. So much were we as one with one another during that terrible time of trial, that mutual compassion filled all our hearts as we struggled to bear our ordeal in the bowels of Kinkasaki's black, forbidding mountain, with some measure of manly British pride.

I was favoured by Our Lord and allowed to live. They were released from their lives of brutalized misery only by the compassionate hand of Death. Each new droplet from my eye is a pearl of remembrance for my fallen comrades.

J.M.

New Mains
North Lanarkshire
October, 1998

Verse, Illustrations and Maps

Illustrations

Page x (line drawing by the Author)
Kinkasaki: JM and John 'Dempsey' Kane run into trouble with 'Frying Pan'.

Between pages 80 and 81
1. Young Yeomen. JM and his brother Richard, 1939.
2. 'B' Troop, The Lanarkshire Yeomanry, 1939.
3. With 'Dusty' Miller, 1941.
4. The SS *Strathmore*.
5. Ahmadnagar, 1941. On the Gun Park.
6. Outside our barrack room, Ahmadnagar.
7. Japanese troops mopping up in Kuala Lumpur, 11 January, 1942.
8. Singapore, 15 February, 1942. The Surrender.
9. 'The Changi Oil Syndicate'.
10. The 'Selerang Incident'. 30 August, 1942.
11. The Kinkasaki Survivors Medallion.
12. The Kinkaseki Memorial, 1997.
13. The entrance to the mine today.
14. The Kinkaseki Garden of Remembrance.
15. JM with Nan, November, 1945.
16. And in October, 1998.
17. JM's copy of the King's letter to all returning Far East Prisoners of War.

Maps

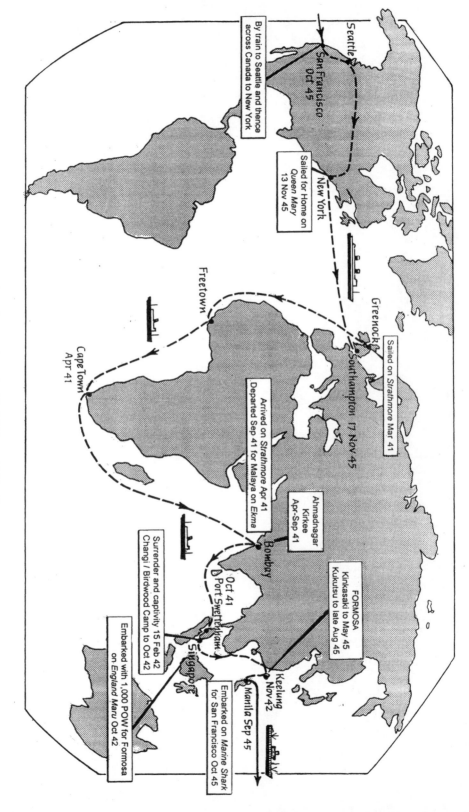

1. John McEwan's World Tour 1941–45.

1

We're No' Awa' Tae Bide Awa'

It was cold and dreich on that memorable morning of mid-March, 1941, as the troop train chugged its way through the damp, smoke-laden mist which enveloped it, slowly leaving the railway siding behind in the rural market town of Lanark.

That train was packed to capacity with Gunners of the 155th (Lanarkshire Yeomanry) Field Regiment, Royal Artillery. The air was filled with the lusty, boisterous singing of the young soldiers who crowded the open windows of the carriages, belting out their regimental battle song '*We're No' Awa' Tae Bide Awa*".

So it was that eighteen months of loving and laughing, trial and tribulation, were thrust behind them as off they set to war, with the fair – and not so fair – maidens of Lanark waving their hands in tearful and sorrowful farewell, with the young – and not so young – menfolk shaking their fists in hostile condemnation, many hurling terms of abuse at those they saw as the despoilers of their womenfolk and calling out: 'Fireside soldier bastards. Hope the bliddy Jerries get yese'.

★　　★　　★

Before the outbreak of war on 3 September, 1939, the former Territorial cavalry regiment had been brought up to strength by local Scots from the towns and villages of Lanarkshire, Dumfries and Galloway. Then, with the transition from horses and swords to field artillery, equipped with 4.5" howitzers left over from the First World War, batches of English, Welsh and Irishmen had been drafted into the

newly formed 155th Field Regiment RA – now a unit of highly proficient gunners, trained to perfection by imported regular officers and
NCOs. So it was that amidst the predominantly Scottish dialects and
accents, the odd interloper could be heard above the din of noisy chatter as all babbled away about this and that . . . of good deeds and foul.

No one knew where they were going and all debated their
unknown future, some suggesting North Africa, claiming that they
would clip General Rommel's wings with their trusty howitzers,
putting the Lanarkshire Yeomanry squarely on the front pages of the
national Press, so burying once and for all the unenviable tag of 'fireside soldiers'.

Above all this noisy babble of boastful chatter, a rough, gritty voice
could be heard, with a heavy Welsh accent that you could have cut
with a knife. 'Taffy' Morgan, a hardy ex-coalminer from mid-Wales,
was having a last go at the local lads back at the railway siding. 'Did
you hear those bloody tartan turnips?' His booming voice dominated
the carriage and its occupants. 'Calling us bastards. They must have
forgot that we left those behind us!' A malicious grin contorted his
rugged features as he voiced his cruel jibe. Still grinning with irreverent glee, he went on: 'Just shows you how ignorant these stupid
haggis bashers are' – his raucous boasting in keeping with the
disparaging expression on his heavy Welsh features. 'Do you know
what Maggie called the bairn? "Taffy" she bloody well called him;
christened him, Taffy Mac-bloody-Tavish. She thought Taffy was my
real name!'

This brutal exposition of past passion with Maggie MacTavish
brought forth more spontaneous ribald mirth from all and sundry at
poor Maggie's expense, with Taffy's coarse belly laugh several decibels
above the rest.

I left the carriage window and squeezed into a seat beside my mate
'Dusty' Miller. 'Did you hear that knuckle-heid on about Maggie?' I
asked in a low voice. I did not want Taffy to hear, he was much bigger
and broader than I. Dusty was a few years older than my own twenty.
'Typical bloody Taffy-dai, Johnny Mac, old chap. All the same, these
bloody Welsh wailers. Only time they shut their bleeding row is
when they are in the land of their bleedin' fathers – six feet under!'
He caught Taffy's eye and waved at him across the carriage with an
ingratiating smile. 'All right Taffy? Maggie OK? Little Taffy OK?'

Taffy was still grinning. 'OK, Dusty boyo! Maggie OK, Taffy OK and me, Morgan the Mighty, OK!' and giving a loud, roaring Johnny Weismuller Tarzan-like cry, a loud undulating, bloodcurdling, trumpeting call, he thumped his battle-dress clad chest with both fists.

We had all lived so close to one another for the last year and a bit that we were well acquainted with one another's faults and failings and were able to make allowances for each other when required. Taffy was no exception. We were all mates now – one for all and all for one – and Taffy had proved a formidable ally in the odd dust-up with the aggrieved citizens we had left behind in Lanark. So each individual's imperfections were tactfully tolerated as we were now united by a common pride in our membership of the Regiment – each of us proud indeed of so great an honour.

*　　*　　*

The clickety clack of the wheels, as they sped over the joints in the rails was sweet music. The dream that I had so often had was at last being realized – we were off to war. I felt the kindling of a sense of importance now that I, a proficient gunner, was on my way to do battle with the enemy – whoever and wherever that enemy might be. Our 155th Field Regiment, with its fine 4.5" howitzers, would surely make short work of anyone who opposed us. These and other youthful and unseasoned thoughts coursed through my mind with visions of future glory.

We left the tall tenement buildings of Glasgow behind us and entered the estuary of the Clyde, the train slowing and coming to a juddering halt at the dockside on the waterfront of Greenock. There we waited patiently to detrain and board one of the many lighters ferrying troops out to the great liners lying anchored out in the deep water of the estuary. As I sat there, reality began to dawn. We were indeed going abroad. To where? To glory . . . or what?

As our turn came to board our lighter, a small Glaswegian member of its crew, with cloth bunnet askew on his greying head, entertained us with this rendering to the tune of *'Bless Them All'*:

Aye ye'll go; Aye ye'll go; whether ye like it or no',
Sergeants and Corporals and WO1s and Fireside Soldiers with
bliddy big guns.

So I'm saying Goodbye to yese all; as on to the Strathmore yese crawl;
Ye'll get no promotion, this side of the ocean,
So cheer up mah lads, bless yese all.

As he finished his disparaging ditty, one of our lads took offence and bawled 'Away ye go yah auld bastard. Ah hope ye fa' intae the bliddy watter'. Quite unabashed, the ancient mariner continued to do his bit for the war effort with some nifty soft shoe shuffling with his well worn tackety boots. Then, with an exaggerated doff of his tatty bunnet and a good natured twinkle in his eye, he 'made a leg' to a rousing cheer from most of us. His timing was perfect – probably because he had gone through the same repetoire for every boat before our own. Even as he finished, we bumped gently against the side of the mighty ship towering above us, which was to be our home for some weeks to come. Looking up, I saw the name *Strathmore* on her bow.

★   ★   ★

The stories of uneventful journeys half way across the world on troop-ships are legion and ours was, in essence, no different from the rest. Learning to sleep in a hammock was both frustrating and hilarious, trying to shave in salt water would have tried the good humour of a saint but the food was infinitely better than that to which we were accustomed from our own cooks back in Lanark and as the great convoy, guarded by destroyers, cruisers and even an aircraft carrier, made its way south, there was much to see from the ship's rail and marvel at – not least our brief call at Freetown in Sierra Leone, where we refuelled and had our first sight of Africa and Africans. Poor Dusty was a very bad sailor and suffered endless misery from sea sickness, made no easier to bear by the sarcasm of our Troop Sergeant, Sergeant Joe Murgatroyd, a regular soldier of many years service, whose mission in life was to lick us into shape as worthy soldiers of the Royal Regiment. Joe had spent some time under the merciless heat of the Indian sun and we all believed that he was not wholly responsible 'up top'. Nevertheless, under his hard exterior, there was, we knew, a heart of gold.

Some days after leaving Freetown, we found ourselves in the

glorious surroundings of Table Bay and the tall, well-built houses and business premises and the massive feature of Table Mountain, told us that we had arrived in Capetown. The warmth of our reception by the people of South Africa, black, brown and white, was something that no member of the Regiment would ever forget.

We were given no shore leave that day but were paraded on deck to be lectured about the customs of South African society and the implacable rule that Black was Black and White was White and never the twain should meet – a rule that we infringed at our peril. I wondered at this intolerance and then, being young and ignorant of the various cultures which made up this vast new world in which we were finding ourselves, forgot about it. Little did I realize there the time would come, all too soon, when we ourselves would be on the receiving end of an intolerance which defied imagination. The day passed and that night I slept peacefully on an open deck under the full South African moon – musing and dreaming of the terrible state in which civilization now found itself, with a world war raging and blood and tears being spilled on the battlefields and in the homes of those who fought.

My dreaming was abruptly shattered by Joe Murgatroyd's booming 'Wakey! Wakey! You horrible lot' and, breakfast dealt with, we got into our clean kit and prepared to march round the great city.

Who could forget that march? As we swung along to the strains of '*Colonel Bogey*', played by a military band at our head, my mind became full of patriotic hysteria and my chest must, I swear, have swelled from its normal thirty-six-and-a-half inches to at least forty. From the pavements to the uppermost stories of the tallest buildings, the people were cheering. Every window was packed and we were deluged with tickertape and flowers, confetti and streamers, of every colour. No royal figure could have experienced a greater sense of exhilaration than did we on that memorable occasion.

We made a complete circuit of the city and, as we began to return, a pipe band from somewhere in front of us put the final gilt on our gingerbread by playing that air that belonged to us, the Lanarkshire Yeomanry, alone – '*Carnwath Mill*', our regimental battle song. This caused such a surge of emotion that even the officers and Sergeant Joe sang their hearts out. When we reached the docks once more, Joe, with a proud smile on his face, strode up and down our ranks:

> Look at yese – like a bloody bunch of nancy boys with yer baggy bloomers dangling. What a bloody awful sight! Even the bloody cat wouldn't drag you lot in.

Then his smile broadened as he continued:

> But I would, you Tally-ho* buggers. You still look like bloody tin soldiers – but ye're made of the right metal, and I'm almost proud to be a Lanarkshire Yeoman too!

With that grudging tribute, he squared his great shoulders and, with head held high, turned on his heel and disappeared up the gangway.

On the following day we were allowed shore passes to go 'walk-about' in the great city – a day forever etched on my memory.

Dusty and I were walking down a wide, well-kept street and Dusty, despite the warnings given us about race relations in South Africa, had just received a sharp warning from a policeman for giving a couple of pretty young black girls the glad eye and a low wolf whistle, when we were approached by a charming and beautiful white lady who, giving us a lovely smile, asked whether we would like to join her and her sisters in their home for supper, adding 'You would both be very welcome'. Noting our surprise, she added, 'It's just our way of showing our thanks for your services against Hitler's oppression'.

'Well', I thought, 'this is our lucky day!' Who could refuse such an invitation from a beautiful woman? Dusty was clearly of the same mind and in no time we were climbing into a taxi which she hailed and heading for the family home in Plumstead.

Miss Patience Owens' home was delightful. Her two sisters at once

---

* 'Tally Ho!' has always been a term associated with the Dumfries and Galloway border areas of southern Scotland. With so many of our regiment coming from Dumfrieshire or thereabouts and the borders being a great area for fox hunting, we knew our border comrades as 'Tally Ho! men' or 'Doon Hamers' [Down Homers to the unlearned Sassenach] ie. those from the south.

made us welcome and feel at home as we went into the dining room, where the table was already laid with a delicious-looking meal. When offered a drink, Dusty and I both opted for South African 'Anchor' beer, being unused to wine. Served in tall, stylish glasses, it was excellent and helped us to relax. As I looked around the room, I could not help comparing this lovely house with the 'single end' in which I had grown up with three brothers and two sisters, my mother cooking over an open fire and the room lit by paraffin lamps. Although I felt a great nostalgia for that home, I could not also help feeling a stirring of a sense of inferiority in that comfortable, stylish setting in which we found ourselves.

My attention was drawn back to the present as Patience asked if we would like to eat now? A young black maid, in a spotless uniform, brought in large plates of meat and vegetables and *rice*. Never having seen rice before except in a rice pudding, I decided not to eat it and Dusty followed suit. Next came a delicious trifle and coffee and cheese. Patience had noticed that we had left the rice and wondered why. What could we do but own up to the fact that we had never seen it served with a main course before? The day would come when we would have given our souls for those helpings of rice.

The beer was now stifling my feelings of inferiority and I thought of the value I had received in exchange for the King's shilling which I had accepted in the Drill Hall in Wishaw on the night that I had volunteered. Dusty rose to the occasion. The sisters, knowing us both to be Scottish, asked for the Selkirk grace. Dusty was able to oblige and received an appreciative response which quite made his day.

After we had eaten our fill, we settled into the comfort of armchairs in their big, airy lounge where big ceiling fans wafted cool, fragrant air around us. I had never before seen such grandeur. Nor had I ever been in the company of such refined and gracious ladies.

The powerful beer was loosening our tongues and our tactful hostesses patiently endured our painful verbal rambling with amused tolerance. To my horror, Dusty began to show all the signs of becoming a little more than friendly with one of the ladies. I quickly rescued him from this potentially disastrous course by rising reluctantly as the clock struck nine to tell Patience that we had to be on board by ten o'clock.

Inviting us back on the following day, an invitation we accepted with alacrity, little knowing that we would by then be at sea once more, Patience took us down stairs and put us in a taxi, which she paid for. We reached the ship with minutes to spare. There stood Joe Murgatroyd, watch in hand. 'Another two minutes and you bevvied buggers would have been swabbing the decks tomorrow', he growled. But the twinkle in his steel blue eyes belied his gruff admonition. Sergeant Murgatroyd was a good soldier who knew when to indulge us a little.

Climbing into my hammock, I quickly fell asleep. In my dreams I was with Patience Owens, mounted on my horse, sword in hand and bandolier slung around my shoulders – back in Lanark once more but ready to defend Patience and her sisters to the death.

★   ★   ★

I was torn from my reverie by Joe's inevitable bellows of 'Wakey! Bloody Wakey!' Tumbling to the deck, I could feel the plunging motions of the ship and the vibrations of the engines. I knew at once that we would never see Patience Owens again. Once more we were a target for any passing U-boat and at the mercy of the sea.

As we sailed into the Indian Ocean, rumour abounded but the plain truth was that not one of us knew where we were actually headed for and no hints were being given. Nevertheless, it was a peaceful period of leisure that we now enjoyed as we basked upon the open decks.

We had been at sea a week when HMS *Belfast* steamed alongside us with her ship's band playing '*I Belong to Glasgow*'. We cheered them and the sailors cheered back. It was a happy little interlude and we felt a great bond existed between us and the crew of that great warship.

On the next day, Dusty and I were up on 'A' Deck when he suddenly pointed excitedly and said 'Land, Johnny Mac. Beautiful, bloody, solid land. I wonder where it is?' Following the line of his outstretched arm, I saw a long mass of broken skyline and agreed that indeed it was land – but where? The barren rocks of Aden? The Sudan? We would soon find out. As we drew closer to the unidentified coast, we could see a scattering of buildings and then what seemed to be a sizable town or city. Then I smelled a strange aroma and Dusty remarked on 'the funny smell'. We nearly jumped out of our skins as Sergeant Joe bawled in our ears:

Funny smell is it? You two buggers haven't bloody lived yet. That is the most beautiful pong in the world. That is curried rice, curried chapattis and curried every other bloody thing. This is Bombay. Good old Mother India.

★   ★   ★

As our grand P&O liner slowly eased its way to the dockside, berthing with a gentle bump alongside the rough edge of the quay, I offered up my personal, silent thanks for our safe arrival and gave thought to the skill of the Captain and his crew who had brought us so far and delivered us in this strange new land, the first signs of which I could now see below me on the dockside, in the teeming mass of dark skinned Indian labourers in their white cotton dhotis and in the proud bearing of the women, in their colourful, spotless saris, carrying an astonishing assortment of earthenware and other containers on their heads without any apparent discomfort. I was enchanted by this busy, multi-coloured sight of which, but for the outbreak of war and the generosity of King George VI of England, I would have known nothing.

My reverie was quickly shattered by the arrival of a group of turbanned policemen who at once began to wield their *lathis*, as I would later discover that their long handled batons are called, on any docker who got in their way or seemed to be slacking in his work. I wondered at the submissiveness of these poor, hungry looking natives as they accepted this treatment without question.

I was getting richer and richer each day in my knowledge of my fellow men and the strange beauty of foreign lands. Now I was in the front row of the stalls, getting a clearer picture of reality, of the all-pervading poverty and harshness amidst the grandeur and glitter. During the months ahead, I would often compare the lives of the Indian labourers to my childhood life in Lanarkshire, where I had experienced a poor, working class background in the miners' rows beside the pits in which my father worked. We certainly knew and suffered real poverty. Luxuries were virtually unknown but as I saw how the poorest Indians lived, in tiny makeshift dwellings, often constructed of cardboard caked with mud with, perhaps, if they were lucky, a sheet of rusty corrugated iron for a roof, I soon came to realize that, compared to these people, I had had a very comfortable child-hood indeed. Had I not seen it, I would not have believed that such hopeless poverty could exist and I felt great sorrow for them. Until then I had always thought myself to be on the bottom rung of life's ladder – but these poor folk were several rungs lower than me.

★   ★   ★

After the Regiment had disembarked, we were taken to a large go-down or warehouse on the dockside where some white women were pouring mugs of tea and handing out sandwiches in paper bags. As I reached the table, I realized that, quite unlike the warm, enthusiastic welcome that we soldiers had received in South Africa, here we were being regarded by the *mem-sahibs* as something untouchable and were tolerated as beggars might have been. Joe's gruff voice sounded in my ear 'Bloody officers' wives; lived the good life for years and bloody years and think of us squaddies as lower than bloody wogs. Bloody stuck up cows'. For the first time I began to understand the caste system which prevailed in this land. My new-found sense of superiority was mortally damaged and I was back at the bottom of the ladder again. The signal from those cold, clear eyes was immediately obvious.

Fortunately, the time had come for us to entrain and we were soon on our way, moving slowly past the *Strathmore* where I saw a sight to gladden any soldier's heart. The Captain and his officers were on the open area of the bridge at the salute as a gesture of farewell. I felt that the Captain was looking directly at me, singling me out for my soldierly prowess and I felt proud to have sailed under his command – but such are the day-dreams of youth.

Some hours later, after darkness had fallen and the intense heat of the day was beginning to cool, we arrived at the ill-lit station of the town of Ahmadnagar. Boarding the waiting lorries, we soon found ourselves in the military barracks which were to be our home for the next three months.

Life for the soldier in India was quite unlike anything he had previously experienced. Sleeping in large barrack-rooms on Indian charpoys (ropework beds) and cooled by the punkah – a large straw mat which wafted backwards and forwards throughout the night, powered by a donkey engine – he would wake in the morning to find himself already shaven by the '*nappi-wallah*' a custom dating back to

Victorian times – at a cost of six annas a week, with Sunday 'buck-shee'. For six annas a day he could have two changes of clothing washed by the *dhobi*, with Sunday again buckshee. His baggy khaki drill uniform, which the long voyage out had done little to improve, was soon smartly tailored by the *dhursi*, who sat on the verandah with his ancient sewing machine, as he worked away for a modest fee. However, all these joys soon began to make a sizable hole in the few rupees paid to the soldier by an ungrateful government and left precious little for any form of self-indulgence.

The great heat, which rose to 120 degrees Fahrenheit by the time the sun was well up, meant that we paraded early for our rifle and gun drill and, after an extended afternoon break, paraded again from 4pm to 6pm. The wearing of topees (or pith helmets) was obligatory and any man found bareheaded in the heat of the day was severely punished, even if only making the short trip to the latrine block.

Three months of relentless gun drill and the eternal striving of our officers and NCOs to exact peak performance from us, saw us leave Ahmadnagar with a proficiency that induced the belief that we were the equal of any regiment in the Army. That belief was confirmed by Murgatroyd J. on the day before we left and was further emphasized by the gift from our officers of a bottle of local beer, known as 'Puggled Panee', apiece. Morale was sky high and we looked forward to the day when we could prove our worth on the battlefield. But what battlefield? We still did not know and most of us thought that ere long we would be heading west again for the Middle East.

The morning we left the barracks, most of the village turned out to wave and shout 'Goodbye, *Sahibs*'. Some of the *bibis* (womenfolk) smiled shyly, especially those who had made a rupee or two out of the more daring lads who, despite the direst warnings on our arrival there, had ventured to 'dip their wicks'. The traders from the bazaar, who, despite our every effort to outwit them, had 'taken us to the cleaners', had also turned out. In truth they had profited little, for our pockets had been lean enough, with our rewards from the Army being so mean. But it had been a great adventure that we had enjoyed during those three months and, indeed, an education.

We all waved back to the *bibis*, the children, the *nappi-wallah*, the *dhobi*, the *dhurzi* and the *char-wallah* and gave them a rousing farewell chorus of '*The Carnwath Mill*'.

For we're no awa'tae bide awa',
We're no awa' tae leave ye.
For we're no awa'tae bide awa,
We'll aye come back and see ye.

Caught up in the spirit of goodwill, a few of us threw our few remaining annas and pice to the children and watched them scramble for the money. It was a grand finale for these poor but honest, well-behaved and pleasant children of the village.

★　　★　　★

It was almost dark when we reached Kirkee, tired and bruised after our long journey in the trucks over the ruts and potholes of the so-called road along which we had travelled. Here, only a couple of miles from the large town of Poona, we were to have a spell of rest before moving on to that unknown final destination. The welcome change from the months of gruelling gun drill allowed us to charge our batteries and we enjoyed the relaxation of football against the local teams – Kirkee United, a side composed chiefly of local 'Wallahs', some of whom, being bootless, played in bare feet. I marvelled at the speed of some of them, reducing our players to wild despair, the more cynical of whom would attempt to halt them by treading on those bare feet – but the smiling Indians always outmanoeuvred them. We applauded their sportsmanship and acknowledged its absence amongst our own fellows who had allowed their frustrated pride get the better of them. Another team that we often played, I remember, was Kirkee Arsenal, made up of white and Indian workers from the local ammunition factory. Some games we won and some we lost, but we enjoyed them all.

Another diversion was the allocation of tickets for the Poona Races. Dusty and I, with a brawny gunner from Kirkaldy, Tam Douglas, were lucky enough to draw the right straw one day and, donning our freshly laundered, well-tailored shirts and shorts, were soon off for the track.

We enjoyed that day, despite being surrounded by well-off Indians, and *pukkah sahibs* and their *mem-sahibs*, who once more radiated that obvious contempt for the 'brutal and licentious soldiery' which had hit us so hard on the dockside in Bombay. But, to our delight, we managed to back a couple of winners at 10/1 and counted out our rupees where we were sure that the snooty white men and women could see us and begrudge us our good fortune, for their very pointed aversion to our presence had ruffled our feathers.

By the time we had had an enjoyable walk around the town, seeing the sights – the Hindu temples, adorned with their religious symbols, and even a nimble mongoose overcoming a deadly cobra, it was time to return to barracks, having thoroughly enjoyed our day.

We were on our way once more all too soon and found ourselves boarding yet another delapidated train. Yet again, the local people crowded the railway line to see us off. There they all were, the United Team, the sweepers, the *dude-wallahs*, and the *bhistis* but no *mem-sahibs* or their *burra-sahib* partners. The Indians had come to recognize us as 'Brithers . . . for a' that' and worthy of their friendship. We returned their shouts of 'Good luck' and roared our 'Tally Ho!s' as the train moved off. As we left, we threw them our football boots, guessing that we would not be needing them again, and belted out '*The Carnwath Mill*'.

*　　*　　*

Once more the question of our destination was the main topic for discussion as we rattled along. Most of us were still sure that it would be in the Middle East. But wherever it was, we were confident that we would give a good account of ourselves with the assistance of our 4.5" howitzers and under the guidance of our by now well-respected officers and NCOs, with Joe Murgatroyd well to the fore in our minds.

It came as no surprise when we realized that we were now back in the area of Bombay. No magnificent *Strathmore* awaited us this time but a diminutive, battered troopship whose name on its battered bow told us its unprepossessing identity – the *Ekma*.

As we left the port and headed south, it became obvious that our dreams of glory in the Western Desert were ill-founded – so where the hell were we going? We simply had no clue. We took comfort from the presence of a battalion of Gurkhas on board – wherever it was to be, at least we would be in good company.

We had not been at sea for many days when we sighted land. A vista of trees greeted us, stretching as far as the eye could see. This was all so different from the barren plains of India, to which we had now grown so accustomed. What strange land was this?

After following the coast for a few hours, we found ourselves at Port Swettenham on the west coast of Malaya. We had reached our final destination at last! Instead of the vast, open deserts of the Middle East, we had now arrived in the jungles of the Far East – a possibility to which we had never given a thought. Life has many surprises and this was certainly one for me. I was getting around the world on a free pass granted by 'Generous Georgie'.

If our surprise at our new surroundings seems naïve, it should be remembered that Japan had not at that stage entered the war and all our thoughts about the war had been centred on the challenge posed by Hitler and his massive German armies, as Britain still stood alone in defiance of that threat.

2

Malaya

We lost no time in removing our guns and equipment from the murky holds of the *Ekma* and left Port Swettenham behind. We headed northwards and eventually arrived at a cluster of wooden huts, set in a clearing on a huge rubber estate near Sungei Patani in the Malayan state of Kedah.

The difference between our present environment and the vast plains of India could not have been more apparent. Here the suffocating jungle of thick rubber trees hemmed us in on all sides. Within this claustrophobic setting there prevailed a most uncomfortable humidity, and we were constantly in a sweat. But being young and hardy – and British as well – we tolerated this with Brittanic stoicism.

An adaptive lot we considered ourselves. This had been hammered into us by our very able sergeants and sergeant majors, who excelled in the military art of moulding civilians into hardened, efficient and dispensable units of war material, willing to do as we were bid without question. Discomfort and hardship was what we thrived on. How else could we have amassed such a Mighty Empire? With 'Bullshit' and 'Blanco', of course, and a lorry-load of bloody sweat . . . and effin' and blinding.

Darkness came! Bedtime arrived at the bidding of the regimental trumpeter's 'Lights Out'. Just before I fell asleep, I listened to the cacophony of jungle sounds; of insects and creepy-crawlies; of jungle animals large and small. I was momentarily startled by the reverberation of Tarzan of the Jungle's yodelling call of the wild.

15

Looking out of the opening in the billet, which served as a window, I was just in time to see Morgan the Mighty, stripped to the waist and thumping his chest with his clenched fists before scuttling back to his billet with a daft Welsh grin on his face. The wild-life became stilled, having apparently taken fright – as had also one terrified young officer who was poking his head through a window with mouth agape, at this alarming occurrence.

In the morning we were up smartly at the sound of Reveille and, after a wash and shave and breakfast, we listened to a lecture from our troop officer. He explained to us that Japan would possibly enter the war and invade the British possessions in the Far East. That was why we were here.

Now, at last, we had discovered who the enemy was to be. They were little men on bicycles who all wore spectacles and were ill-equipped for war against the likes of us. Such was the nonsense that was imparted to us that morning as we listened attentively. In our unworldy naïvety and with our utter faith in our superiors, we believed it all. We were also somewhat relieved that we would not have to fight the dreadfully efficient German Army, the 'Huns', but rather these little 'no-accounts' from Tokyo. We patted ourselves on the back at our good-fortune. We would show these 'wee men' the road back!

Such was our working-class gullibility. But even then I could not help dwelling on the fact that our preparation for war had all been in the wide-open spaces of rural Lanarkshire and the even wider plains of India, yet here we were in the confined entanglement of the eternal jungle and rubber plantations of Malaya. It didn't make much sense to me, but then . . . not to worry. Our backroom boys knew their stuff. Mr Churchill and his aides back in London and our own very efficient generals right here would have everything in hand. They would know the score. So, not to worry.

The town of Sungei Patani was nearby and, having the rest of the day off, I joined Dusty Miller and some of the other lads in the billet on a visit there and on the way saw how the rubber was extracted from the trees. A small, metal container was attached to the trunk, some v-shaped notches were cut into the bark and a narrow metal guide was stuck at the bottom. The whitish sap travelled and dripped continuously along this and into containers.

Indian, Tamil, Chinese and Malayan labourers collected the latex and carried it to a waiting truck. They seemed to have a good working relationship and a common tolerance. I could not help comparing this with the policy of Apartheid in South Africa, the effects of which I had seen in Capetown. I was still young and had much to learn of the big world, but was learning every day. I was also extremely confused at times! To each his own! Who was I to tell other people how to run their countries?

As we walked, monkeys were swinging in the trees above our heads, contemptuously unconcerned at our presence. During my time in Malaya I came across scorpions, centipedes and evil-looking spiders, as I had in India. I had always had an interest in wild things. We continued towards Sungei Patani and later there was a rustling in the branches a short distance from us. A great, hairy creature was hanging by one arm and one foot, gazing down at us with a quiet indifference. It was an orang-utang – an old man of the woods. After it had spent a short time looking at us, it swung from branch to branch and was soon out of sight.

Our visit to the town was brief as we had to be back at the camp for dinner. Nevertheless, we partook of such unheard of delicacies as fried banana. We had fresh coconut with the top sliced away and a straw to drink the milk, and lemon tea which an old Chinese woman provided for a few cents. We tried and enjoyed slices of pineapple and tried all these luxuries at prices which even a British Soldier could afford.

As in India, there were brothels with smiling, welcoming girls, both young and old, of many nationalities and colours, offering their bodies at bargain prices. Since their customers were soldiers, bargain prices it would have to be, or no prices at all. We remembered Joseph Murgatroyd's graphic description of the 'perilous parasol' treatment should 'a packet' be acquired and declined to accept the discounted terms.

Next day came the order to 'limber up', with the guns and limbers hooked on to the quads (the vehicles which towed them.) We soon found ourselves on the open road, heading northwards, and eventually arrived at the town of Jitra, not far from the Thailand border. Here we unhooked our howitzers and the limbers and began to prepare gun positions, for action should these little upstarts from Tokyo insult us with their presence. 'The cheek of them! We would show them!' I thought, with smug complacency. Such is the bravado of ignorant youth.

We toiled and sweated to clear patches of thick, jungle trees and undergrowth. We cursed and profaned those muscle testing obstacles that we encountered. We rested briefly as the quads came to our assistance with cables attached to stubborn trees and dragged them from the ground. Great cheers would ring out at this.

Here, too, at Jitra we met the rest of the 11th Indian Division and the other regiments and battalions of British, Indian, Commonwealth and Malay soldiers who would fight by our side should the Japanese really invade Malaya. It was comforting to know that we were not alone in an uncertain situation.

The East Surreys and Leicesters and some Indian infantry too seemed to be preparing against attack. An anti-tank regiment joined in with the same urgency as ourselves. I now felt that danger was imminent. The Play Days were over! This was for real! I could feel it in my bones.

We applied ourselves energetically to our gun emplacement, NCOs and officers too lending their weight. Just before dark, we finished our task to the satisfaction of the Battery Commander and boarding our transport, we headed back to our camp at Sungei Patani.

After a few words of appreciation of the day's labours from our officers, and with a satisfying meal inside me, I welcomed the trumpeter's Light's Out. I wrapped the blankets around me and fell asleep '. . . perchance to dream sweet dreams of yesteryear.'.

The following day we were on parade for inspection by our Commanding Officer so plenty of 'spit and polish' and 'bullshit' were called for. Prior to the CO's arrival, there was the usual 'shufti' by little Lieutenant Anderson. He strode along our open order ranks with Sergeant Murgatroyd, who made his customary belligerent observations to this one and that – deservedly or otherwise.

Next time, Gunner Ponsonby, stand a little closer to the bloody razor! And you, Miller, you look more like a bloody camel than a soldier of the King! Get your bloody shoulders back – and your chest out – and your head up! You, Douglas, what's that bloody awful evil-smelling grease

you've plastered your hair with? Bloody, poofy Brilliantine is it? Bloody
Air Force you should be in – or the bloody WAAFs!

And so Joe would dish out his normal verbal abuse whilst 'Wee
Andy' would pretend not to notice – but with a (scarcely observable)
smile on his florid face. The rest of the gunners and NCOs would be
grinning widely at each target of Joe's raillery. We all knew him well-
enough by now and fully understood that each one of us would get
the edge of his tongue when the opportunity presented itself.

Suddenly, the sound of a motor-cycle could be heard, weaving its
way through the rubber trees. Colonel Murdoch came into view
astride a BSA 500cc motor bike and slithered to a stop in front of
the Regiment, which was quickly called to attention. He dismounted
and, adjusting his monocle, surveyed his ram-rod stiff troops with a
proud air.

We didn't see an awful lot of our CO but respected him for his
down-to-earth attitude towards us. We respected too his authoritative
manner. He stood there wearing his well-polished eye-piece, tapping
his right leg with his leather-bound riding crop as he looked us over.
With a touch of personal pride in his voice, he addressed us after
ordering 'Wee Andy' to stand us at ease.

'I must say I'm mighty proud of you chaps. I've been watching you closely
and come to the conclusion that I am the lucky boss of the finest bloody
field regiment in the British Army. So keep up the good work, lads and
we'll give these little buggers from Japan the toes of our boots if they dare
to meddle with us.'

He turned away then and after having a few words with the troop
officers, strode smartly to his powerful BSA and swung his leg over it.
Kick starting it first time, he roared away through the trees again,
waving his riding crop in farewell salute and bellowing 'Tally-ho!
Tally-bloody-ho!'

That was our colonel. He had loved his cavalry, because of his love
for riding and all that went with it. He loved the Yeomanry and its
troopers; the manoeuvres in the beautiful rolling hills of the Scottish
borderlands. Now his consolation prize was the machine astride
which he sat. It had two wheels to replace four legs but still a saddle

to sit on and handlebars to replace the reins. For all of the difference in our backgrounds he was 'one of us' and was never averse to showing it. He was quite willing to speak man-to-man with us as the occasion presented itself and truly we respected him for it. Colonel bloody Bogey? . . . Our Colonel Murdoch left him in the shade.

Days came and went quickly now with the constant journeys to Jitra with our guns, and with drill orders in the surrounding rubber estates and jungle. For all our previous training in the open country-side, we quickly adapted to this new terrain with the restricted movement that it permitted. As we surmounted our problems, we grew in confidence and proficiency. We became deft and professional, capable of manoeuvering our howitzers in the thick woodland. At times, when occasionally a gun would get stuck in a muddy hole, the nearby East Surreys and the Leicesters would encourage us with good-natured heckling, and would cheer when the gun was eventually hauled out and into position. This growing closeness of a kindred spirit welded us more solidly into the framework of the 11th Indian Division and instilled a sense of pride and unity. It also promoted a confidence for the indeterminate future and whatever it would hold for us. 'Wha daur meddle wi' me?' I was thinking again.

November, 1941, came and with it a pleasant surprise. Our regiment was given a break and moved to Ipoh, further south. Here we lived it up, enjoying ourselves as best we could with the pittance that our government paid its soldiers. We saw the sights of this quite beautiful town, with its, quite large, population of Chinese and other races, including the native Malays. But the month of November passed all too quickly and we returned to the north once more to Sungei Patani.

We were soon back to the daily grind with no let up in the gruelling gun drill. Joe Murgatroyd yelled his crude blasphemies at us and his original expletives as we strove to satisfy his demand for even greater efficiency at our tasks. It seemed impossible for us to satisfy him, but we nevertheless sweated and laboured incessantly with this goal in mind.

Rumour was rife now but as the first week of December ended we received word from military headquarters in Singapore that the Japanese 25th Army was on the move. It was at sea and heading south in the direction of Malaya itself. A 'jildi move' followed as officers and men rushed about with great urgency.

On 7 December, 1941, we travelled at speed to Jitra, where we took up our position, near the Thailand border, to await the coming of the Japanese, should they really invade Malaya. As yet we had no idea that Japan had attacked Pearl Harbor that morning or that Britain would declare war on the Japanese barely twenty-four hours later.

Any complacency I had felt up to that point was now gone. As we lined up the howitzers with great speed and assembled our shells and cordite charges in readiness, I felt a great tenseness gripping me. The time that we had been waiting for, and training for, has come at last. This was the time to excel at the job in hand and redeem ourselves. The tainted title 'Fireside Soldiers' was hanging in the balance. It would soon be an obsolete disparagement. But . . . and the thought persisted, at what price? What great sacrifice might be exacted from us in payment for the removal of the demeaning title bestowed upon us back home. As I watched, my comrades I could see signs of anxiety at the threat which lay just over the horizon. The 'wee men' were beginning to grow very big.

Darkness came and the hours slipped by with an eerie chill hanging around us and a silence so profound it could almost be heard. I was sure that the thumping of my heart would certainly be within earshot of nearby gunners as they crouched at their guns, seeking reassurance from the stout metal. Conversation was practically nil as the seconds, minutes and hours of 7 December, 1941, were left behind.

We awaited the first signs of hostilities on the morning of the 8th. Rain began, adding to our discomfort. There were many oaths and curses of the age-old variety but many which had never before been introduced to the listeners. We gunners huddled together on that fateful, damp and dreary morning and did our best to catch an hour or two of sleep, with the gun sergeants staying awake lest some emergency arose. We were not to sleep for long.

News came that the Japanese had landed troops at Kota Bharu on the north-east coast of Malaya and that fierce fighting was in progress. They had been engaged by troops from the Argylls, the 5th Field and the Indians of the 9th Indian Division. This news was followed by further news that General Yamashita, with elite troops from the 25th Army, had also set foot on Thailand at Singora and Patani on the east coast. He had been totally unopposed there by the Thai military for the Bangkok government had just signed an agreement with Tokyo giving the Imperial Japanese Army right of passage through their territory. His units were now moving quickly across country to cut off our own north-western positions on the Thai border. Sleep was the least of our worries now and sergeants bellowed out commands to their gun crews while the officers checked relentlessly to ensure that all was ready for a sudden attack. The waiting was now over and the gunners fully alert, talking and shattering the quiet with the loud clanging of breech blocks, as the howitzers were loaded with their squat thirty pound shells. We prepared for our first taste of action against the contemptible little army of cyclists from the Land of the Rising Sun.

We would blow these little buggers off their bloody bicycles and scatter the pieces to hell with our weapons of destruction if they should be so impertinent as to come near us. They would be very sorry that they had had the cheek to sully our colonial soil with their uninvited intrusion. As I thought these things, I was, perhaps, making an attempt to raise my own morale because, now that bloody contact with the enemy was inevitable, I could feel a surge of shivers disturbing my self-constructed stiff upper lip and the growth of goosepimples. A degree of mortal fear was taking hold in the face of morbid imaginings of the consequences of what I was engaged in. My veneer of bravado was gone. I realized that, for all the worldly education I had received on my, paid-for, travels, there were some aspects that could very well be done without.

Afflictions such as I was suffering at that time were part of the wonder of creation, I realize: the gift of 'The Big Man', Himself. The antidote is also provided for our attacks of spiritual and mental melancholy. It is time, itself. As the minutes ticked away, my normal optimism began to re-assert itself and drove away my depression. I began to feel very 'British' again and ready to fly the jolly old flag once more for King and country! I felt my shoulders begin to broaden again and the imaginative capacity of a youthful mind took over.

Then came consternation all around as the air was filled with the sound of heavily laden bombers high above us in the shrouding darkness of the dark clouds. They announced to us the arrival of the Japanese. They brought destruction to people and property somewhere along their flight path. There were obvious sighs of relief as the last of them passed overhead and faded into the distance; southwards in the general direction of the island of Singapore.

2. The Malayan Battle Areas, 1941–42.

This was our first contact with the enemy. They had been so near, directly overhead, and the rain-laden clouds which we had cursed so roundly just previously had given cover to us and possibly saved us from inglorious annihilation. Had it been a moonlit night, the pilots would surely have spotted us and blotted our copybooks. Perhaps clouds did have silver linings. Tonight's most certainly had, I thought. My chance for a Victoria Cross had survived for the gory days ahead. How terrible it would have been to come all this way and to be killed by a bomb without the chance to fire even one bloody shot.

As we listened to the Thud! Thud! Thud! of high explosives in the distance, we knew that what we had missed was falling on some other unfortunates. The Japanese were leaving their calling card en route for Singapore, with the towns of Alor Star, Sungei Patani, Ipoh and Kuala Lumpur the bloodied addresses.

Thus did our war in the Far East begin. Here we were on the threshold of battle at last. Soon we would be forever rid of the title we hated. Strangely, for all my imaginings of impending glory, the anxiety about my own well-being of body and soul had lingered.

Darkness faded as dawn approached and word filtered through that our infantry, The Leicesters, the East Surreys and some Indian troops had been engaged in a fierce battle with the Japanese. The Japs had been supported by tanks and planes and our men were retreating and suffering heavy casualties. The news was demoralizing.

Even more demoralizing was the further tragic news, from Kota Bharu, on the East Coast, that the invading 18th Japanese Division, led by Major-General Hiroshi Takumi, had also successfully forced the defending British and Indian troops to retreat. Both sides had suffered heavy losses, the gunners of the 9th Indian Division sinking a couple of enemy troopships while the Argylls and other defenders had given a good account of themselves.

But they were up against an able leader in Takumi. In the event, the surrounding jungle saved them from complete annihilation as they fled before the battle-seasoned soldiers of His Imperial Majesty Hirohito and his warlord Tojo. No mention had been made in the reports of 'Little men on bicycles'. The Japanese had brought tanks with them. We had not! Our own military strategists had 'boobed' with the omission of these very necessary weapons and had placed us at a grave disadvantage. The odds, it seemed were against us.

24

Then, as the Japs came down upon us from the interior of Thailand, we were, ourselves pitched into battle on our own north-western front. Our beloved howitzers hurled salvo after salvo of high explosive shells in an attempt to stem their relentless advance and to give our troops time to re-organize. In that we succeeded, causing confusion among Yamashita's soldiers – for the moment anyway.

We now had a brief rest before more frenzied Japanese attacks came in, as they sought to disrupt our new defensive positions with machine gun and rifle fire; with bombardment with mortar and with cannon. I experienced for the first time the stimulating uncertainty of battle and became acutely aware of being 'in amongst it'. I had found out at first hand the true meaning of Field Artillery – being on the field of combat beside the infantry and so to be available to lend a hand in time of need. More learning I could have done without. My Royal Patron's investment in my education was paying off.

We held the Japs at bay for four days. The infantry made a stubborn resistance and we made a contribution with direct hits on tanks and by constantly producing devastation within their ranks and denting their morale. The incessant, bloody, action was taking its toll, however, with almost no rest or sleep for any of us. We dealt out death twenty-four hours each day and plastered the enemy with shell fire. The barrels of the guns became almost too hot to touch.

Sergeant Murgatroyd ensured 'no rest for the wicked' as he wakened any gunner who nodded off with a heavy hand. He and the officers swore at us ruthlessly and goaded us into further attention to our barbarous duties. We 'effed and blinded' in response and renewed our slaughter because they were the cause of all our troubles. 'Bastards; Jap Bastards; Bastards, Bastards, Bastards . . .' and so the venom poured from us.

We were mere machines now and slaves to the ever-increasing needs of the howitzers. It was as though they were the masters and we the servants. Our duty was to keep them alive, to nourish them with deadly shells and to satisfy their greed for the twists of obnoxious cordite which fuelled their ability to hurl those shells far and wide. We did as we were bid and diligently appeased their appetite with the fodder they demanded.

Fire – Load! Fire – Load! Fire – Load! The action went on, and on, and on! My initial fear, stemming from first contact, had left me now.

I was part of the urgency which prevailed all around me. Breach blocks clanged open and shut and shells hurtled away to bring carnage to the recipients. The need for survival brought complete dedication to the task in hand.

We obeyed the strident commands of gun sergeants, and suffered the constant stinging fumes of spent cordite charges as they dissolved in the sweat of our brows and, dripping thence into our eyes, they blinded us. This prompted more tirades of belligerent oaths. There was the continual shattering percussion of the high explosive charges in the breech blocks. The sound assailed our eardrums. It suggested to me a scene from Hell as gunners staggered amongst the smoke-shrouded guns to supply them.

We were hungry too. The rumbling from our bellies was unheard because of the greater rumbling all around. We were given sustenance at longer and longer intervals. It seemed that the cooks, far to the rear, were allergic to gunsmoke and Japs. Occasionally they would arrive with a 'fast-food' hand-out of a can of bully beef and some hard-tack army biscuits. But who could blame them for keeping their distance? We had not seen a British aircraft since the start of the Japanese in-vasion. The few old and obsolete Brewster Buffalo fighter planes, at Kota Bhan were destroyed by the Japanese within the first few hours of the fighting there. We were out-numbered by the able and sea-soned Japanese troops and, while they had tanks in support, we had none.

We were in deep trouble and knew it. Japanese pilots cruised just above tree top level, knowing that there was no opposition and nothing to fear, as they dropped their bombs and sprayed their bullets at will. We could actually see them looking out of the cockpits and smiling at our chaotic situation. General Tomoyuki Yamashita must have been smiling too.

★   ★   ★

Meanwhile the two great ships, the *Prince of Wales* and the *Repulse*, had been steaming southwards to support us, with their complement of four destroyers and not one aircraft to support them. On 10 December, off Kuantan in the South China Sea, they had been sunk by squadrons of Japanese torpedo and high level bombers which had been dispatched by Rear Admiral Matsunaga commander of the 22nd Air Flotilla in Saigon.

The *Repulse* had her rudder blown to pieces by a direct hit and fire and black smoke had belched from within her stout metal hull. She sank with her guns still blazing within an hour of attack. The destroyers, *Vampire* and *Electra* manoeuvred bravely to rescue survivors from the sunken *Repulse*. There was an unexpected display of compassion from the Japanese pilots as they signalled to the destroyers that they had done what they had to do and that *Vampire* and *Electra* should go ahead with the task in hand. The Japanese pilots deliberately ignored the two rescue ships and concentrated on the crippled *Prince of Wales* which was already in a bad way. She was listing badly to port and already sinking. The Japanese pilots allowed the destroyer *Express* to come alongside her to pick up shattered survivors. Amidst the awful horrors and bloody carnage of total war, there *can* appear acts of compassion.

★   ★   ★

In the early hours of 13 December, Yamashita launched a massive full-scale attack upon us with fresh troops. Our line broke in utter disorder with our infantry retreating – they were suffering from battle fatigue and in a state of confusion. Indeed, large numbers of Indian soldiers fled through our gun emplacement in terror and panic, so ferocious was the Japanese onslaught. After them came the Leicesters and East Surreys, dishevelled and demoralized. So reduced were their numbers that they were henceforth to be known as the British Battalion.

It was a nervewracking situation for us. It seemed that we were entirely on our own now with the infantry behind us and I felt, as most of my comrades did, that we had been 'thrown to the lions': The dreadful chill of fear for my life had me in its grip once more as we manned the guns and continued to harass the enemy with high explosive. 'What a bloody state of affairs,' I thought 'Abandoned by our fellow men'. I could not understand this, having absorbed the traditional British values (or old-fashioned piffle – depending on your point of view). I scorned the stampede of the Indian soldiers and, with my heart beating at top speed within my breast, I continued to respond to the urgent bellowing of Sergeant Joe Murgatroyd, who cursed and blasphemed as he drove us to get on with the job. So I, too, cursed and blasphemed as well, with none but myself to hear and with the comforting thought that no one could hear the racket that was being made by my overwrought 'ticker'.

Soon I had cause to feel ashamed for even thinking that we had been left in the lurch as into view strode a number of Gurkha soldiers, led by their white commanding officer. These fearless Nepalese soldiers injected new spirit and reassured us as they took up position beside each gun with rifles and kukris at the ready and not a hint of panic on their light brown faces.

I relaxed a little and was certain that I could hear loud sighs of relief from the rest of my comrades at the presence among us of these small but utterly reliable soldiers of fortune from the heart of the Himalayas. Some fatalists will have it that the 13th of any month is 'unlucky for some'. I uttered a silent prayer that I would not be among that number. I understood also that our infantry had made their way to establish new defensive positions and that we were a necessary buffer to allow them time to re-organize. We continued to blast away at the advancing enemy, laying down a barrage of barbarity. We had to hope for yet another intervention from Lady Luck which would decimate the ranks of the Nipponese invaders.

I was suddenly gripped by a profound terror as, from the thick jungle in front of me, Japanese soldiers came charging with fixed bayonets, screaming 'Banzai . . . Banzai' while a mad-looking officer wielded a Samurai sword as he led this Kamikazi assault.

This was the moment for guns to fire at random over open sights at the oncoming, screaming hordes as pandemonium ensued amidst the clamour of bloody combat. Every gun was in frantic action, expelling shell after shell in quick succession. Some scored direct hits on individual Japs, blowing them into pieces; others hit the trees behind showering the area with devastating fragments of British steel. There was much letting of warm Japanese blood.

The brave Gurkhas too, were doing their valiant bit and dealt swiftly and efficiently with the Japanese soldiers who had the mis-fortune to break through. The invaders were hacked to death with razor-sharp Kukris, bayoneted or shot with Lee Enfield .303 rifles. At last piles of dead and dying Japanese lay on the open ground in front of our howitzers.

Through the smoky haze from spent cordite, I saw Taffy grapple with the Japanese officer. Taffy wrested the fearsome-looking Samurai sword from his grasp, swung it with deadly intent and decapitated his squealing victim with his own ceremonial blade. In the most bizarre act I had ever seen, Taffy then brandished the sword above his head and did his own 'Banzai' with a bloodcurdling rendition of his favourite 'party piece', the Tarzan-style jungle call.

It was an awesome sight, that place of bloody carnage, with the soldiers of the Japanese Emperor screaming in pain and terror as arms and legs were torn away from bodies by the deadly shells hurled into their midst by desperate, perspiring gunners. Others lay on the ground, faces contorted in pain and screaming with agony and distress at the knowledge that their shattered bodies had been mutilated beyond repair.

Then the silence of the grave settled over the area as the savage Banzai charges from the fringes of the jungle were halted and the order to cease-firing was given. With the heroic Gurkhas guarding our rear, we lost no time in hooking up guns and limbers and departing the scene of our victory; leaving behind the dead and the dying from the Land of the Rising Sun. We had given a reminder, we thought, to General Yamashita that the 155th Field Regiment was not to be trifled with. He would surely remember it and the lethal sting in its tail.

The battle for Jitra was over and our victory of the last few hours was of little account since the Japanese were still advancing and would soon catch up with us again and make amends for their recent failure at the wrong end of our tireless, merciless guns. Our forces were retreating in bewilderment and disorder and I thought that things were looking grim. I felt a twinge of shame and of perplexity as we fled from the relentless attacking Japanese. I wondered where their bicycles were as I hadn't seen any yet.

I nevertheless felt proud of my regiment. We had earned our moment of glory by stopping the enemy in his stride. We had fought and won, for a little while anyway. We were worthy of the title 'Soldiers' without the, now unwarranted, prefix 'Fireside'. I saluted Taffy and saluted too Lieutenant Anderson, who had stood beside him firing his revolver at the 'Banzai bastards'. He was not very tall but had one big heart made of British oak, an officer to be proud of.

Darkness fell and utter confusion reigned once more. The road southwards was thronged with dishevelled and disheartened troops, still dazed by the hammering they had taken from Yamashita's soldiers. Like all of us, they were reeling from excessive fatigue from the past days of continuous battle. Progress was slow and frustrating. It was imperative to establish another line of defence further south, in an attempt to halt the steady progress of the enemy. At last we reached our new position, thankful for the cover of night, which prevented the Japanese planes from annihilating us all on the road we had just traversed. It had been packed with soldiers.

What a bloody guddle! What a mess the brass-hats had made of it! My mind was racing with quick anger! Rule Brittania! No wonder we were losing what was left of our Empire and losing it fast. Perhaps our generals had been too long in the hot sun of the Far East and their brains were addled. Or perhaps they didn't have any in the first place. Either way we were in it up to the bloody neck and the night was made much darker by the giant, black cloud of depression which hung over us all.

I knuckled my forehead to Heaven again and was just half-way through five 'Hail Marys' when the gravelly voice of Joseph Murgatroyd interrupted my plea for deliverance from our predicament. I was back to Earth once more.

'Action Rear!' his voice boomed. We promptly obeyed the commands he gave and began to work with a will at getting our howitzers lined up and ready for another exchange with the Japanese when they came within range. Joe was on hand, urging us on with vigorous and unsavoury expletives as the remnants of the British and Indian troops straggled past. We waited and waited and waited with sagging upper lips and faint hearts for Tomoyuki's vanguard to catch us up.

We did not have long to wait since Yamashita was not an individual who liked to hang about and attacked once more. The infantry dribbled back through our guns, with us doing a fast follow-up. The tanks and planes at their disposal lent great impetus to Yamashita's Japs and ensured them certain victory.

It did not help our misery to hear that Major-General Hirosho

Takumi was advancing across country from the eastern front with the intention of cutting us off. This would indeed have brought a speedy end to the already mortally wounded Malayan campaign. We required a fast move south now to prevent this catastrophe. Morale within the 11th Indian Division was not too high – to say the least. The Japanese Generals had the ball at their feet and were scoring goals with every manoeuvre.

What a mess! No planes and no tanks! Our only major warships, the *Repulse* and the *Prince of Wales*, had been sunk by the Japs at the beginning of hostilities. Did Churchill really think that warfare still involved trenches and 'over the top'? Perhaps he was still fighting the First World-War? Perhaps he was on the wrong continent? Or perhaps he should have retired and let a more up-to-date candidate take control and save the lives of many young men of Britain and the Empire who would be sacrificed needlessly in this chaotic bloody morass of military mismanagement.

The Japs were now landing troops along the coast to our rear at will, having captured Penang and commandeered a multitude of small craft. By this strategy Yamashita ensured that he caused the maximum confusion in our ranks and that we could be attacked from front and rear and from the flanks. We were continually on the move southward towards Singapore with panic and frustration as our travelling companions. Our movement was a grotesque parody of hop-skip-jump, with actions going on on all sides and Singapore getting nearer all the time.

Kampar Valley, south of the town of Ipoh, was reached and here we took up positions and we gave a good account of ourselves. We repelled Yamashita's forces for the first time since the beginning of the Japanese landings at Kota Bharu and, of course, our own 11th Indian Division's engagement of them at Jitra in the north-west. This gave some lift to our flagging morale.

Our force now comprised: the Argylls, the British Battalion (Leicesters and East Surreys), the Indian battalions, the stout-hearted Gurkhas and some British artillery regiments, of whom not the least was the 155th (Lanarkshire Yeomanry) Field Regiment. Together, we succeeded in thwarting each attack and the Japanese suffered heavy casualties in hand-to-hand fighting, with our gallant infantry battalions, who decimated the enemy's superior numbers with rifle and

Bren–gun fire and ferocious bayonet charges. Our own contribution to the victory was a crucial one as we slammed shell after shell into the mass of Japanese soldiers, with terrifying consequences for them.

Exhausted as we were, having had little rest during the past weeks of action and movement, we sweated at our guns and felt the return of our old pride and the reconstruction of a shattered self-esteem. I remembered a thought from, what seemed, long ago. 'Wha daur meddle wi' me?'

A welcome feeling of exhilaration elevated me as we held our ground against the stubborn Japanese advances. The words of patriotic songs flowed through my mind. 'Britons, never, never, shall be slaves'. These words accompanied the incessant roar of our howitzers as they blasted the life from the Japanese and let them know who were the masters.

Morale was now so high that I actually expected that we might, perhaps, push forward, and I was not alone in that thought. I felt I had grown another six inches and might rival the Iron Duke in military might. I imagined myself riding his sturdy horse, Copenhagen, into battle.

Hogmanay, the last day of the year, arrived and, as we approached midnight, huddled around our guns, we were commanded by Lieutenant Colonel Murdoch, whom we greatly admired, to celebrate the New Year. We were to do so with a gift for Yamashita by firing twelve shells at the enemy in the manner of the twelve strokes of Big Ben at midnight in London which would usher in 1942. On the stroke of midnight we carried out his order and delivered our deadly gift with grim satisfaction.

But there was no singing; no 'Guid New Year tae yin an aw' for this was neither the time nor the place. We had no idea what 1942 would bring for us. Our future looked decidedly shaky at this stage. We could only wait and see.

We held our position in Kampar Valley for four whole days without giving up an inch. At the end of that time, to our surprise, orders came to withdraw. We were southward bound again and ordered to form a new line of defence at Slim River. We reached it on 7 January, 1942, my 21st birthday. It was to be a sad birthday and a sadder one for the regiment. Our morale had taken another dent from the order to withdraw. We had retreated again just when we had begun to believe that the tide was turning in our favour. The depression of spirit which had lifted seemed to sweep down again. Even our much loved, unfriendly Sergeant Murgatroyd looked dismal. He had been so uplifted by events at Kampar Valley that he had forgotten to speak harshly to us. Now he was back to giving us the rough edge of his tongue as normal. Strangely, this made us feel better as it gave us something to divert us from the possibility of darker days ahead.

Our new position was to be ill-starred. The Japanese lost no time in pressing forward with fresh troops, with the usual air cover and tank support. One of our guns went into action almost as soon as the first tank appeared and crippled it with a well placed shell but was then blasted itself by intense fire from cannon and machine-gun fire which killed the sergeant and wounded the other unfortunates manning it. Worse was to follow. Our CO, Colonel Murdoch, arrived on his motor-cycle and was caught in the devastating hail of fire from the disabled tank. He lay sprawled across his sturdy mount while its raised rear wheel spun madly as if itself in the throes of death, just as the hind legs of a stricken horse will often thrash wildly about as it dies.

Tragic it was but a fitting end for a fine leader. He died, while along with his regiment in the thick of battle, his monocle in place and his riding crop clutched tightly in his hand. The nearest thing he could get to one of his beloved cavalry horses, his powerful bike, had proved a worthy steed with him to the end. Its bloodstained, khaki coloured, petrol tank had received several bullet holes and petrol gushed out. The bike was never used again.

That is fate. There are no favours for those of high station. The high and the low must accept the cards as they are dealt. Prince and peasant are equal and both may equally dread the arrival of the Ace of Spades. Colonel Murdoch's death only confirmed this.

Another hasty retreat followed, with more unsuccessful skirmishes with the wily encircling Japanese. We met them at Batu Pahat and again at Yong Peng and Kluang. It was at Kluang that another strange 'first' occurred.

Our signallers were often alone as they maintained the lines of communication between the infantry and the guns. One of our men shouted in alarm as he saw a pair of feet, in army boots, partially hidden in the long grass which grew in the monsoon ditch along the road-side. On closer inspection it turned out to be one of the signallers, who had been dispatched earlier to do some maintenance checking. The signaller, whom I shall call Willie D, was lying in the ditch on his back, holding the ends of some cable which had been cut. It was evident that he had taken fright when he had found the violated cables and had simply 'frozen'. To say that he was happy to see friendly faces is something of an understatement. The terror in his eyes as he babbled incoherently about the severed cable showed that he had worked out that there must be Japanese in the vicinity.

We calmed Willie down. We, too, shared his apprehension. Every one of us knew by now what fear could do to even the best of men. We had the chilling thought that they might even be watching us at that very moment from the cover of the thick jungle foliage and might be about to annihilate us all. It was not a comfortable thought.

As we stood, uncertain what to do, two small men on bicycles appeared and made to pedal past us with a patronizing grin on their oriental faces. They were stopped and Willie Williamson, a Yeoman from Sanquar, near Dumfries, searched them. Their fate was sealed when wire cutters were discovered under the saddles of their bicycles. They were taken back to our gun-site after being bundled unceremoniously into a truck. They were discovered to be Japanese soldiers dressed in the singlet and shorts favoured by the local natives – and were two very frightened men. Since they were not wearing uniform, our troop officer shared the common view that no mercy need be shown to the trembling saboteurs. He authorized their execution, which was carried out expeditiously. Bullets from our rifles felled them as they tried to flee from us and reach the protection of the surrounding jungle. They would cut no more wires.

Those were the only 'small men on bicycles' that I saw during the entire Malayan Campaign.

Yong Peng, Batu Pahat and Kluang were left behind as the Japanese attempt to cut us off continued. Our luck held and we beat them to it, although often only by the skin of our teeth. Eventually the mainland itself was left behind in the possession of the Japanese, who were still unopposed in the air and at sea, as they had been throughout.

Singapore Island now became our last place of defence from which we could retreat no further. We were hemmed in by the Pacific and Indian Oceans which held us like rats in a trap. There was no escape for us! We were done for – the end was nigh.

Even lowly gunners and privates knew that the battle for Malaya and for the island of Singapore had been lost some time ago back on the mainland. An unbelievable sight met our eyes. It was now a couple of days short of the end of January, 1942. Incredibly, a large number of fresh troops were being landed at Singapore's docks and were identified as the British 18th Division. They had come to work a miracle. Well it was long past miracle time. We felt sorry for those newly arrived, smartly blancoed and clean-cut young soldiers.

Whoever was responsible for not diverting them to Australia or some other location capable of being defended was guilty, as far as I was concerned, of a war crime. That was how I saw the future of Singapore.

These young men had no experience of battle and many of them were newly recruited from civilian life. Like the mountain of war equipment which was abandoned to the enemy during the Malayan Campaign, and which littered the length and breadth of the Malayan mainland, these men were abandoned to the invaders. Many of them were taken prisoner without having fired a shot and would die miserable deaths in captivity. More 'Churchill supplies', as the Japanese had labelled our deserted 'goodies', after the past ten weeks of constant retreat.

In Singapore we capitulated to the Japanese generals and their armies on the afternoon of 15 February, 1942, with the awful and shameful burden of surrender hanging around our young shoulders and our prospects for the future uncertain.

There were many tales of past atrocities committed by the Japanese against the Chinese and those stories did nothing for our peace of mind. Our fate was not in the lap of the Gods; it was in the hands of the Japs.

Ironically, our final position in the city of Singapore was in the immediate vicinity of the infamous Lavender Street. It was a street of ill-repute which had a range of brothels, both cheap and pricey. They offered the services of willing prostitutes from Malaya and China, from other Asian lands and even some from Europe. It was a fitting last stand for us. We were, after all, the Lanarkshire Yeomanry/155th Field Regiment, lecherous and treacherous opportunists, as some aggrieved cuckolds from the County of Lanarkshire might label us. And perhaps the accusation had a grain of truth. But now we had no thought of

35

dalliance with these lovely and lusty ladies, because all had changed. Here in Lavender Street the mighty Malayan dollar ruled and no favours were granted without it. And since no dollars had greased our palm during the last three months, our pockets were empty. The local ladies did not operate on credit and so 'That was that', as the saying goes.

In any case, the pleasures of the flesh were far from our minds. Much closer was the preservation of the flesh. There would be no 'Jiggy-jig' on this grey day and what we did not yet know was that there would be none either for very many even greyer days to come.

A death sentence hung over us. We might never see Lanark again. Perhaps the Japs would do away with us all? I became morbid and despondent. Perhaps the young men who had stayed behind in Lanark and given us a vindictive farewell on the morning we left the railway siding would be twice as happy at an unexpected bonus. It was the bloody Japs that got us, not 'the bliddy Jerries'.

Now we might have to alter the words of our regimental anthem, *'The Carnwath Mill'*.

'We're no' awa' tae bide awa'

Perhaps we were.

So Much for Glory

Is this the glory that we sought,
When for a shilling we were brought
By George of England, and his aides?
Not knowing soon we'd be in Hades.

Not knowing as we took the 'oath'
To fight for King and Country, both
Would leave us high and bloody dry,
In far off lands to bloody die.

Abandoned when we lost the fight,
'Twas, 'eff you Tommy, I'm alright',
By bungling 'Brass', with 'Sorry Mate'.
Then left us to our bloody fate.

In jungle, and infested swamps,
And soul destroying prison camps,
Where cruel guards, and strange disease
Combine to bring us to our knees.

As daily we are all paraded,
Bare foot, naked and degraded.
Skin and bone – or very, very
Bloated . . . those with berri–berri.

And the lads with dysentery,
Squatting forty times a day
On smelly bore–holes, thick with fly,
Knowing that they're doomed to die.

So much for Glory that we sought;
Young foolish dreams have come to naught.
For Nippon won the day instead,
And soon we'll all be bloody dead.

3

Changi

The Japs kept their distance that fateful day in February, 1942, and this instilled in me some hope that we were to be spared the fate described by some of the gruesome stories that had been going the rounds as to what could possibly happen to us. We dared not sleep that night, however, lest they stole among us and plundered our persons, lock, stock and barrel. Better to be safe than sorry . . . so we kept whatever weapons we had in readiness – just in case.

In the morning, we were lined up by our officers and marched away from our location, with tearful farewells from many of the prostitutes who waved to us from their windows. They had genuine pity in their eyes – and seemed unmindful of any danger to themselves. It was a serious possibility that the concern that they had for us should, perhaps, be reserved for themselves. This token of unexpected compassion from an unexpected source made me deeply appreciative of my fellow man. A lesson, too, was learned that a parcel should never be judged by its wrapper. Who is to know what priceless treasure it may contain? These lustful ladies of the Orient would often be despised, even by those who partook of their fleshly charms for a few Malayan dollars. Yet, within their breasts beat hearts that differed not at all from any other person's – no matter their rank.

My education was expanding with the passing of each eventful day and I felt richer spiritually for it. I waved back to the girls and asked God to look after them – for I had the idea that their new masters, the Japs, would lose little time in patronizing these mansions of the 'madams' and claim their 'pound of flesh' without due payment of the ducats.

We reached the open coastal road and headed in the direction of Changi, on the east of the island. It was here that the full import of our demeaning defeat by the Japanese was driven home to me.

I could not believe my eyes as I saw that the road – to the front and to the rear – was filled with bedraggled, battle weary troops and wondered where all of these thousands of soldiers had been during the fighting. Then I remembered the shiploads of squaddies who had been needlessly sacrificed by our warlords back in England, by allowing them to land at Singapore when the bloody battle was over and done with, just in time to be taken prisoner. That act of gross foolishness was to cost many of these poor unfortunates their lives.

And now there was the added humiliation of being stared at by the groups of Japanese soldiers who lined the road, smoking their cigarettes and staring at us with open contempt from the shade of the coconut palms. Flags of the 'Rising Sun' fluttered everywhere in the breeze and hammered home to me the message that the bloody sun had set for us all.

An hour or so later, a break in the coconut groves revealed a high walled, turreted building and into Changi prison, we, the 155th Field Regiment, and some of the other troops from the main, endless column were directed into its forbidding confines. As I entered the massive iron studded gates I had the uneasy feeling that the Japs had selected this particular place of punishment for the Yeomanry in retaliation for the pounding to which we had subjected them with our howitzers during our battle engagements.

The huge gates clanged shut behind us and we were crammed, five men at a time, into cells that were meant for single occupancy. These were to be our quarters for the next five weeks, with the concrete floor our mattress and a bucket in the corner for our convenience . . . and who could complain that it was not convenient, it being so close to hand?

So this was the start of our captivity, with many hardships to come in the dark and ominous future and the added humiliation and frustration caused by seeing former comrades – sepoys who had 'turned their coats' manning heavy machine guns in the surrounding guard turrets along the prison's high walls. The prison was packed to capacity and, as a precaution against dysentery, we got rid of the 'bog' buckets and dug latrines in the exercise yard. This necessary decision by our MO's deprived us of whatever little modesty we had left. Desperate candidates for the use of these open trenches would squat 'mooning' themselves – a dozen to the row – as they did what they had to do. Swarms of bluebottles and cockroaches added to the discomfiture as they continually 'bombed' the exposed posteriors, causing indignant consternation and much 'effing and blinding' by the unfortunate squaddies.

This provided a welcome distraction from the increasing hardships being suffered by the present inmates of Changi prison. Good-natured crudities about the misery and misfortunes of their defecating mates would be hurled inconsiderately and occasional coarse laughter would rend the air while the targets of this humour balanced precariously on the edge of the latrine, suffering the ever present danger of falling in.

But this is the true grit of the British Army. Into the very darkest of tunnels a glimmer of light is brought. Rough and ready when they enlist, or are 'press ganged' in time of need, the naturally inherited coarse, but lighthearted, humour is further polished by 'Colonel Bogey's finishing school' and its hardened Regular Army NCOs. Hard-boiled eggs we are – but with soft centres. Well, most of us anyway.

Rice was now our daily diet, but never enough of it. We had a handful of boiled rice two or three times a day, depending on how much the Japs issued to us. This was supplemented by a mess tin of watery soup, which our restricted cooks provided. So the hard times were with us now and eternal hunger our constant companion, with slim waistlines becoming markedly slimmer.

So we had to bear it – but without the grin – and hope that Mr Churchill would get off his fat arse and rescue us from the debilitating situation into which he had landed us. We were well and truly in the soup and, hungry though we were, it was of a kind not to our liking.

A week passed and the queues for the latrines were getting longer due to the fact that as the trenches began to fill up, the continual heat from the blazing sun intensified the awful stench from the contents. This attracted more and more cockroaches and bluebottles, which then contaminated the rice in the nearby cooking area. This, in turn, caused acute diarrhoea to flourish amongst us and there was the day and night humiliation of attendance at the primitive toilets, hoping that you would 'make it in time'.

It must be remembered that these were the most primitive of conditions, without even the basic availability of toilet rolls – or any kind of paper for that matter. It was truly a fine mess that we had gotten into and I still marvel at how we coped with so degrading a situation. But circumstance is the dictator of conduct, so we managed as best we could and adapted to the problem in true British Army tradition.

Each night, as I lay tightly wedged between the bodies of my fellow prisoners on the cold, hard concrete floor of the cell, I tortured myself with the thought of the wonderful meal that Dusty and I had enjoyed in Plumstead, Capetown. I remembered our timorous approach to rice as part of the main course, as opposed to rice as a pudding, and moaned quietly, as my empty stomach craved for such sustenance. Food, food, food, was the predominant talk among us now, with all else of little importance. Once again it had been shown that the prevailing circumstance would dictate the relative importance of all things. An empty stomach is not easily denied.

Little did I know then that this state of being was to afflict me for the next three and a half years. Little did I know then that many, many among us who had avoided glorious death in battle would be doomed to extinction by extremities of hunger and slavery in prisoner of war camps. (Glorious death would have followed had we fought to the last man, as Mr Churchill had apparently decreed, from the depths of his dugout in London). With hindsight, all of us, I am sure, would have agreed to fulfil Mr Churchill's wish. But the future is not ours to see and perhaps that is just as well.

The Japs made themselves conspicuous by their absence until the end of that first week then, suddenly, a squad of mean looking soldiers appeared at the jail and commandeered around fifty of us for a work party outside the prison. I was included in the party and was inwardly jubilant at this chance to escape the claustrophobic, demoralizing stink of the place. A breath of fresh air, I thought to myself, and I am certain that all the others chosen felt the same . . . and perhaps a chance to obtain something for my aching belly, should the opportunity arise.

42

We were issued with shovels and chunkals (similar to heavy garden hoes) and marched out of Changi jail, with our guards scowling all the while and snarling '*Hakko, hakko . . . Speedo, speedo!*' at us. They emphasized their brusque commands by occasional prodding with the butts of their rifles. And now, with this unexpected, hostile behaviour of our escorts, I had a momentary foreboding that the time might come when I would wish I was back within the protection of the unhealthy walls of the jail – blue bottles, cockroaches, evil smelling latrines and all else.

After being hustled through dense groves of coconut palms to the constant unfriendly demands of '*Speedo, speedo!*' from the Japs, we eventually emerged from the shadow and cooling shelter of these trees, and found ourselves on the hot sands of Changi's coastline. Here, we were halted momentarily and divided into five groups of ten. Each squad was positioned at intervals along the sand, and put to work digging deep, wide pits. I wondered, a little apprehensively, (remembering the tales of the horrors perpetrated by these same Japs against the Chinese) if these bloody holes could be for ourselves and the rest of our muckers back at the prison?

Grisly thoughts, indeed, but I was not alone in my dread. Quiet murmurings from my comrades conveyed to me that they also were having visions of butchery in the offing. I offered a plaintive plea to my Holy Father in heaven to hear my cry for mercy and save me from the hands of these cruel savages, these bastards. Then I had to crave His gracious pardon for uttering such a word in my earnest request.

Isn't it strange how, in situations of impending doom, normally irreligious persons, such as myself, will bend the knee in earnest supplication and cry for help from Jock Tamson, or from other favoured supreme and spiritual beings. We shed our cloak of independence and we grovel, like the beggars we are. We recognize – as we usually do in these situations – that we are mere mortals, with an 'axe' ready to fall.

It was to our relief and, at the same time, to our horror that we found that the large, deep holes we had dug were not for us, but for other poor unfortunates. A truck, crammed with fearful, and tearful, Chinese civilians, had just arrived at the side of the road which ran alongside the beach. These people were ejected forcibly from the truck by screaming, laughing, Japanese soldiers. They were made to run down the sand towards the ruffled waters of the sea. As they ran, terror stricken, from their tormentors, one of the soldiers who had remained on the truck opened fire on the fleeing Chinese with a British Bren gun which must have been captured by the Japanese during the fighting.

It was a cold blooded massacre. Terrified men and women, some, indeed, mere boys and girls in their teens, entered the incoming tide in a desperate, but ultimately hopeless, quest for survival, only to be mown down by the spraying bullets from the machine-gun. They wailed and screamed as they died, with the blood from their mutilated bodies staining the salt water a gory red. It made a fearsome spectacle. We stood, hardly believing what we were watching, but with the grim realization that we were in the hands of barbarians of the worst kind and with a growing dread as to what lay in store for us, should they take umbrage at us.

We were not allowed to speculate for long. Our guards, grinning with sadistic evil, made it very plain to us that we were to go into the sea, bring the dead bodies to where we stood and then dump them into the holes we had prepared. To give urgency to our grisly task, they helped us on our way with their hobnailed boots and the butts of their rifles bellowing yet again, '*Hakko, hakko! Speedo, speedo!*' These words of haste were to be imprinted on our minds for the rest of our lives. I ran and stumbled my way to the water's edge, awestricken by the nearness of this dreadful atrocity and petrified by the wanton slaughter of these poor Chinese civilians. I watched in horror as they bobbed about in the undulations of the oncoming tide, their clothing stained bright red with the continual oozing of blood from their wounds. Some who were still alive were threshing around in the deeper water as they fought to fend off attacks by sharks attracted to the scene and made more daring by the profusion of blood-spattered human flesh floating everywhere I looked. The air was filled with the screeching and squawking of encircling, swooping seagulls as they vied with the opportunist scavengers from the Pacific Ocean for the odd, tasty morsel that chanced to meet their sharp eyes.

A terrible scene of devilish carnage; of man's inhumanity to man; of brutality and callous savagery which should be beyond the scope of the lofty, intelligent, 'should know better' highest creation of our Maker.

44

But why should I have wondered? Why should I have been surprised at this mind-shattering scene of the destruction of innocent men and women? History has made it clear that, of all the life forms on earth, the most cruel and deadly species is *man*. He can strike terror into the hearts of the ferocious beasts of the jungle with his cunning. It is man who has the capability to reign supreme over all on earth but too often abuses the powers that God has bestowed upon him. Such is the unpredictable life we live. We are a mixed bunch of beings, good and bad; and Good does triumph over Evil at the end of the day . . . Well mostly.

As I gazed in shocked, stupified immobility, a movement immediately in front of me caught my attention and I saw the arm of a young Chinese girl in her teens beckoning me with feeble effort. Her head was barely visible above the shallow water she lay in and instinctively I waded towards her, moved to action by the imploring light in her frightened brown eyes. Reaching her, I saw that the flimsy dress she wore was soaked by the blood from a wound in her breast. I was filled with compassion for her, so helpless and panic stricken did she appear. I stooped and gathered her into my arms, holding her gently to myself as I tried to ease the pain she was so clearly suffering from her terrible wounds.

I was deeply shocked by the appalling situation that surrounded me and felt frustrated and inadequate. I had no idea how to deal with the dreadful circumstance of the moment. No nightmare could ever be as terrifying as the profound reality that I was involved in at this particular time of my young and inexperienced life. No book of exaggerated, wild fiction from the lending library back home could ever be as unbelievable as the scene of devastation around me, as I stood in the blood stained water at Changi and gazed into the eyes of the girl I cradled in my arms. I saw in her eyes a silent cry for help.

Her pretty face was streaked with blood and it seemed that she was incapable of speaking as she continued to stare at me, mutely conveying her plea for release from her tragic plight. I realized that I could not be of much help to her as I listened to her painful gaspings for the air that her punctured lungs were unable to contain.

She was mortally wounded and, as I held her close, I could feel the sporadic shuddering within her breast, shattered by bullets from one

45

of our own British machine-guns as the Japanese soldiers stood laughing. I could feel too, the faint beat of her heart as it faltered within her broken chest and knew that she was dying fast. Young though she was, I was sure that she, too, realized that time was running out on her. I held her fragile body closer to mine as I sought to comfort her in my own limited way. I attempted to penetrate the innermost reaches of heaven, with my heart and soul, crying out for assistance in this, my hour of greatest need. Not, this time, for myself, but for the brutalized young girl I had – by the hand of fate – become attached to in such a manner.

'Tis not for mere mortals to know what lies in store in the future – a bloody good, job too. If they did, suicide would seem an attractive way out of an unbearable life and the cemeteries would be filled to capacity.

I heard her moan and did what little I could to alleviate her suffering, embracing her with compassion and could only utter the words that I felt were so inadequate as I gazed at her painwracked face, 'I'm sorry – I'm sorry . . .'

As I stood there, with the bloodied tide lapping around my ankles, I asked Our Lady to intervene. Even as my prayer was uttered, I knew full well that the young girl was soon to depart from this cruel life, so far had she gone, and that my plea for spiritual intervention would be in vain, but I was desperate, and tried again.

She closed her eyes then, and appeared to go to sleep. At that moment I was brought back to reality as a nearby Japanese soldier came at me and lashed out with his clenched fist, catching me on the side of the head and making me almost fall with the girl in my arms. I caught my balance and saw the vicious Jap bastard pointing to one of the mass graves, into which some of our men were already toppling dead and mutilated Chinese bodies. I got the message clearly, that if I did not get going, then I would be into the hole in the sand too or, at best, in for a hammering. I had no choice but to continue with the gruesome task in which I was involved.

I cursed the whole of the Japanese nation under my breath as I stumbled up the short gradient to where the gaping jaws of the pit in the ground awaited my reluctant offering. I stopped at the edge, unable to complete the grossly inhuman act forced upon me. I felt a cold numbness grip me, and a sense of immense guilt at the look of wounded accusation in the gentle brown eyes of my desecrated young Chinese girl.

She lay absolutely limp in my arms as I cradled her violated young body close to my own and felt the tragedy that had engulfed her affect me also. A surge of uncontrollable emotion took hold of me. Tears from my own eyes fell upon her soft white cheeks and mingled with those she had shed herself. I imagined that I saw the flicker of a smile of silent understanding soften her terrified features. I was full of frustrated remorse, at my inability to comfort her with some token of Christian solace; or Buddhist; or any other appropriate consolation. I could only appeal to My Lord and Lady above once more to fill the gap which I was incapable of closing. Then I closed my eyes and prayed my earnest prayer, 'Hail Holy Queen, Mother of Mercy. To Thee do we cry . . .' I could not finish my silent plea for mercy as, at that moment, I knew the pain of a tacketty boot thumping into the small of my back and I was catapulted through the air with the girl still clutched to me. We landed on top of the pile of dead and dying bodies which were strewn all around. With the cries of terrified anguish from the mutilated carcasses filling my ears, I did my best to keep the weight of my body from inflicting further punishment on her already defiled flesh. Once again full of guilt, seeing the look of reproach in her tear-filled eyes at my failure to save her. A great shudder went through her, as she breathed her last and closed her young eyes forever.

There was nothing else I could do for her now. I laid her limp, desecrated body gently on top of another Chinese woman and, with the depraved Jap who had put the boot into me a few minutes ago screaming at me, I scrambled from the mess of bloody outraged flesh beneath my feet and continued with my grisly task of retrieving more ravaged corpses from the sea and tipping them into the nearly-filled grave.

We were now finding the remains of corpses roped together in groups. They had apparently been taken out to the sea days previously and were partly eaten by the ever hungry sharks and other ocean predators and were now in a sickening state of bloated green and black and bluish decomposition. As before, we were hampered in our unenviable task by the screaming seagulls, as they swooped amongst us to appease their appetites, tearing strips of rotting flesh from the bodies as they bobbed about in the contaminated water. It was a terrible experience, at first hand, of utter carnage and fiendish butchery by human beings on fellow humans. It was an experience that would remain with me for the rest of my life. My 'King's Shilling' was buying for me slices of the 'cake of living'. I would have preferred that the 'icing' had not been blood red and the filling so very tasteless.

The day's ghoulish work over, we were lined up, counted and marched back to Changi prison, very glad to be back within its tall walls and away from that first taste of the brutality of which our captors were capable.

Next day, Taffy Morgan was with me on another 'beach party' and, whilst dragging abused bodies from the polluted water, I noticed that when the guards' attention was elsewhere, he was furtively busying himself with the decaying corpse of some poor Chinese fellow. Unable to believe my eyes, I saw the pliers that he held, and that he was pulling gold teeth from the mouth of an eyeless, bloated carcass. I voiced my abhorrence at his cold blooded act on the poor fellow with 'Bloody hell! Taffy! Bloody, bloody hell!'

He looked at me and grinned, 'Bloody money these are, Johnny boyo.' He opened his hand and showed me another two teeth. 'This is Fu Man Chu's good turn for the day. Poor bastard doesn't need them anymore.' He grinned his barbarous grin once more and stuffed the teeth into his pocket. But what he didn't realize, yet, was that someone else had witnessed his gruesome act of robbing the dead – albeit that it was done with thoughts of barter for food and survival in the days to come.

The nauseating day's work finished at last, we were lined up, as usual, prior to our return to Changi prison's unsanitary confinement. As usual, we were subjected to the regular brutal prodding of rifle butt and fist as the guards made us number off, and number off again, to satisfy themselves that all were present and correct, before we were brought to attention and marched back to our overcrowded cells. But this time we didn't move off right away, as the thick-set, mean looking sergeant in charge positioned himself in front of Taffy. '*Anatawa, dammi, dammi,*' he snarled at Taffy and, patting his own trouser pocket, intimated to my stupid mate that he wanted to know what Taffy had in his.

Taffy, now somewhat worried, pretended ignorance of what was demanded of him – and was promptly and viciously felled to the ground by a quick, ferocious 'one-two' of a left fist followed by a right one. '*Nanni-ka, dosta*?' The Jap stood over the stunned Taffy, screaming like a demented rhinoceros, putting the hobnailed boot in and gesturing to him to get to his feet. Taffy got the message, scrambled up unsteadily and produced the gold teeth, which were snatched from his hand by the Jap NCO to the accompaniment of '*Dammi, dammi. Bagerro,*' and other Nipponese condemnations. The sadistic NCO turned away then, with a final barrage of Nipponese at poor Taffy. He put the gold teeth into his own pocket and spoke to one of the guards who instantly moved in on our bruised and still dazed mate. He gave Taffy 'one for the road' with the butt of his rifle, hard on the front of his brow, gashing it badly and sending him reeling.

Taffy was on the ground once more and bleeding from the treacherous blow to his head. Dusty Miller and I lifted him up and supported him all the way back to the prison with our brutal guards prodding and pushing us at '*speedo, speedo*' time en route, the staggering, stumbling Taffy continually muttering, 'Bastard – bastard – bastard' through the clouded semi-coma which affected him. It chanced that one of the guards heard his muttering and, with lowered brows and suspicious enquiry demanded '*Nanni – nanni bastardo?*' Dusty saved the day by assuring the guard that '*bastardo*' meant 'good – *joto*' and the gullible fool nodded his bullet head in contentment and left us alone.

Eventually the 'beach parties' stopped. After another three weeks, Jap guards appeared inside the prison and we were lined up and with our hastily collected belongings and cooking utensils and so on, marched out of the prison and finally reached Birdwood prison camp further up the Changi coast. This was to be our new abode for the next six months. It was much better than the crowded conditions we had experienced at Changi, with plenty of open space within the perimeter of barbed wire. The wooden huts, too, with enough floor space to sleep on were a welcome change from the cramped five to a cell situation we had left behind us. So this was one answer to my silent prayers.

As before, there were no toilets, so we acquired long handled metal boring tools from somewhere and the 'bore holes' came into being.

Two rows of holes in the ground 18 inches in diameter by 10 feet deep, with a total of twenty primitive, bottomless latrines to serve the needs of the camp. So, here again, we were somewhat better off, although the queues were just as long as they had been back at the well attended trenches of Changi. There were a lot more prisoners here than there had been there.

Here, too, all modesty was thrown to the winds as we had to squat down with the usual accompaniment of dive bombing bluebottles and cockroaches as they competed with each other for whatever was on offer around the proximity of exposed behinds. Yet, unwelcome as they were, these horrible creatures in our midst played their part in adapting themselves as substitutes for absent toilet facilities, as paper in any form was not available and 'dock leaves' were in short supply.

And it was here, as these scurrilous scavengers bombarded us, that the 'borehole' rumours originated, as squaddies squatted on their hunkers and told of things that they had been told by someone else, who had been told by someone else (from a reliable source). In this way, lowered morale was given a temporary lift. Here again, as back in Changi, the agonizing dilemma of the diarrhoea and dysentry afflicted was made into one of our standing sources of humour, as they hopped about, waiting for an unoccupied borehole in order that they might relieve themselves.

'Ten tae wan Muirhead disnae make it,' some sympathetic joker would bellow as Gunner Jock from the 5th Field pranced around in acute desperation. This grim humour would apply to Gunner This and Private That; and Corporal This and Sergeant That; with a total absence of malice aforethought. Then someone else would chip in with, 'Ten tae wan then MacDuff. You're on,' and there would be a hearty round of applause, and boisterous congratulations, when Jock Muirhead or some other victorious 'outsider' did make it.

Such is the camaraderie of the Army. No quarter given where none is expected, but usually underlying such brutal verbal exchanges there lurk concerned hearts of gold – twenty four carats.

One very extreme case of humiliating disaster at the borehole came about one morning, as one distraught and frantic soldier attempted to beat another desperate candidate to a vacated borehole. He slipped on the wet grass. He disappeared feet first, down the murky depths of the circular latrine, screaming his head off. The lucky lad who had lost the race, just managed to teeter to a stop at the very edge of the opening.

Uproar and callous merriment ensued with someone shouting 'Gunner Farmer's hit the target,' and another yelling, 'You mean *shit* the target.' And so the abuse went on. But notwithstanding the unfeeling hilarity, rescue was prompt for their unfortunate comrade. A grimy, knotted rope (which hung on a nearby post for just such an emergency) was quickly lowered to him and even more quickly pulled back up, with the plastered, evil smelling gunner hanging onto the end of it.

In circumstances such as those we were in, the poor fellow's plight provided some welcome distraction from our own miseries of hunger and despondency, with budding poets amongst us composing master-pieces of ridiculous, disgraceful verse about the unsavoury incident. But no ill-will was intended for 'King Pong' as the unlucky guy was dubbed, now and forever more.

The rice ration was as bad as it had been in Changi with our handful of boiled rice and some watery soup to wash it down, so eternal hunger was our constant companion. We talked endlessly of finding the means of securing extra rations of rice and, strangely, the bore-holes came to figure in this plan.

My two floorspace companions now were old mates – John (Dempsey) Kane, an amateur boxer in Civvy Street and Arthur (Trumpeter) Smith, another dependable, hardy lad from the Clyde Valley in Lanarkshire. During a visit to the borehole, Dempsey (as we knew him), came to learn of barrels of oil that were stored at a defunct 15" gun emplacement about half a mile from the camp. Thus was a seed sown that would, perhaps, grow into the means of alleviating the constant pangs of hunger that assailed us.

Dempsey had a plan. Our cooks were forever complaining that they had no light during the dark of early morning to cook the rice. There was no electricity in the camp. He proposed that we should leave the camp some dark night and steal some of the oil at the gun site. If successful, we would make a deal with the cooks – a small can of oil each day, for some extra rice. They could make a lamp of sorts with an empty can, a piece of string, or cloth, for a wick and the oil we

51

would give them. We three agreed to have a go if the cooks should accept. With visions of extra nourishment for our thinning waistlines, we gave Dempsey the go-ahead to sound out the cook in charge and a deal was struck – a mess tin of rice for a can of oil each day, with the rice shared among us. We would chance our luck, and our lives, for the good of the cookhouse – and more importantly – for the good of ourselves. A dangerous, daring scheme it was, so we swore the 'Musketeers' oath of allegiance: 'One for all and all for one.' And one dark and moonless night, as the camp slept, the three of us wriggled our way under the barbed wire and stole swiftly and stealthily along the railway lines that led to the gun site.

Trumpeter was at the rear, lugging an empty ten gallon disinfectant drum that would occasionally bounce against the metal rails with a boom like thunder that reverberated through the silence of the night. After one of these 'booms', we became aware of the lusty singing of a Japanese patrol in the near distance. Dempsey swore at Trumpeter for the noise he was making with the can. Trumpeter swore back at him saying he 'couldnae help it,' and I swore too, beneath my breath, hoping that the dense coconut palms would provide enough insulation to muffle the noise that we were making. Now the dangers involved in our perilous escapade were driven home to us, as we realized that we were in 'no man's land' and were in peril of our lives. We threw caution to the wind and hastened onwards on our mission of 'buckshee rice' with the urgency of mortal danger giving Olympic fleetness of foot.

The gunsite was reached without mishap and we lost no time in descending the iron ladder which led underground to where the oil was stored. We were accompanied by the sound of the empty drum bouncing off every bloody metal rung as Trumpeter lowered it down. Dempsey and I found the large barrel of oil and quickly filled the drum with the precious liquid. With the sound of a Jap patrol in our ears, Trumpeter hauled it to the top with the two of us following. Speed was now uppermost in our minds. We were filled with the urge to get back to the safety of the camp with our precious cargo for the cooks and for ourselves. We sought escape, with the plunder, stolen from under the noses of the enemy. We didn't hang around, with each of us taking it in turn to 'hump' the now heavy drum of oil. The drum was cumbersome and caused much stumbling and staggering as we tripped over the sleepers and the metal rails of the railway. Each of us vied with the others to give vent to the most foul and abrasive cursing at the object of our mishaps. I remember that it was a three way draw! Each of us was equally competent in the dubious art of using the full range and power of the Anglo-Saxon additions to the English language.

At last we reached the barbed wire of the camp. With labouring lungs and aching arms, we crawled under it, unmindful of the occasional barb which pierced our bodies as we hurried to be on the safe side of it once more.

Into our hut now and, worn out by our recent efforts, we hid our spoils as best we could. Having given thanks to the Almighty for answering our desperate prayers for success in our foray into enemy territory, it was such a wonderful relief to lie our bodies on the relative comfort of the rough wooden floor of the hut and pull our blankets around us. Then, sweet dreams of some extra soggy rice in the morning from the cooks, in return for our supply of oil, and perhaps the odd fag from anyone who had such to barter with, for a ration of 'liquid gold'.

And so it was that the 'Changi Oil Syndicate' came to be, with the profits of acceptable merchandise shared between us, with food in any shape or form given top priority in exchange for our 'liquid gold'. A dangerous, perhaps foolhardy, adventure, with the very real threat of instant death in the offing – all for a few extra grains of rice or the odd 'coffin nail'. Well, real hunger is a real incentive for chancing the 'throw of the dice' and one has to experience real hunger to appreciate fully the taking of chances. An empty belly can, at times, make a brave man out of a craven coward. Circumstance is the great dictator of all that we do, or do not do. Was our enterprise bravery, with applause for heroes filling the air? Or was it just a plain, youthful disregard for the consequences, which is to be discouraged? The plain truth of the matter is that dire need drives the human to actions he or she would not normally undertake. We needed food desperately with which to keep our bits and pieces in relatively good working order.

We gave the cooks their oil and received a full mess tin of soggy rice in return. This we split four ways, including our Welsh mate Taffy in the split. We enjoyed every precious grain in the knowledge that we had earned it, albeit by an act of gross stupidity, or an heroic foray into enemy territory (depending on how you viewed it).

Like the splendid and much admired Rolls Royce car which is given loving care and attention as well as fuel to keep its wheels turning, so it is with our own bodies – even more splendid and admirable by comparison. Food and water are essential requirements for good health and survival. In our present predicament, every little grain of rice was vital.

Another day of humiliating captivity had dawned, with the POWs queuing up for their paltry portion of rice, joining the never ending file of men waiting at the spartan ablution facilities and visiting our unique latrines, the bore holes. Desperate customers still vied with one another to claim vacated positions at the latter, but were now doubly careful in their approach, lest they suffer the fate of King Pong.

Constant hunger had taken such a toll on us by this time that our ribs could easily be counted and our hip bones too were now prominent. Things were looking grim and I was of a mind that no time could be as bad as these hard times. Eternal hunger had us in its grip and we were powerless to help ourselves. But the future was still to come and there was no way I could know then that the day would arrive when I would look back at those 'awful bloody times of unparalleled hardship' on the island of Singapore and wish that I was still there.

However, it is in the present that we deal with our unpredictable lives and we make of it what we can, come what may. We have no knowledge of what lies around the dark and dangerous corners in the days to come. As we wend our way through the intricate, enigmatic maze ahead of us, we hope that we will find good fortune at the end of its tortuous passages. Some will falter and come to grief by the wayside; others will stumble and stagger blindly on forever. I wanted to keep going.

At this period of our POW life, the Japs were leaving us alone, and for this we were more than thankful. We remembered, only too well, the terrible crowded conditions of Changi prison and the abominable beach parties. The most dreadful memory for me was of the dying Chinese girl I had held in my arms and of the silent reproach in her terrified brown eyes. More than fifty years later, I still feel a weight of guilt for my inability to bring comfort to her. The accusation in her eyes will haunt me forever.

I remember, just as well, the evil, grinning Japanese who machine-gunned those poor, defenceless people and I damn them to the fires of hell for ever and ever.

Taffy was not in the same hut as Trumpeter, Dempsey and myself and was still suffering from the effects of the bashing he had received at the hands of the guards. He was more often than not morose and would mutter frequently about Maggie and little Taffy. We kept an eye on him and gave him his share of our 'leggy'* rice and this always brightened him up a bit.

Nothing is forever and, after a few weeks furtive enjoyment of the extra rice from our cooks, the empty bottom of the oil drum made itself known and our buckshee rations came to a full stop. 'No bloody oil, no bloody rice,' the cooks informed us – so that was that. A crisis was to hand.

We three held a special meeting and, by a show of hands, and under pressure from empty bellies, decided to brave the wrath of the Japanese patrols yet again and replenish our stock of valuable oil. It was at this time that our officer in charge (The British Officer-in-Charge) posted a notice informing us that anyone caught outside the barbed wire would be shot on sight. We had already assumed that this was so, so it made little difference to our plan of action, although it made us all the more determined not to be caught. Our sortie into forbidden territory would be made in obedience to a higher authority still, our rumbling insides.

We waited until the moon was at its lowest fractional crescent and, as the rest of the camp slept, eased ourselves under the barbed wire once more. Moving quickly for fear of being caught, and shot, we sped for our objective, thankful for the thick blanket of darkness that shrouded us.

We arrived at the gun site and squeezed ourselves under the high metal fence just in time to hear a Japanese patrol approach from the cover of the coconut palms. Terrified, we looked for a hiding place and, spotting a discarded, tattered tarpaulin, crawled underneath and

* POW – speak for 'extra'.

55

lay there. We made ourselves as flat as we could, hardly daring to breathe lest the Jap soldiers, who were now close by, would hear us.

I sweated and sweated as I had never sweated before. And I prayed, and prayed as I had never prayed before. And I shook with mortal fear, as I had never shaken before, as I listened to the Japs talking and laughing just yards away on the other side of the fence. It was as though I had been abandoned by my mates, so quiet and still were they, as we lay under that foul smelling tarpaulin, fearing discovery by the enemy. We feared, too, an end to the oil – and an end to ourselves! I wished that I could transform myself into a mole and burrow deep into the muddy, foul, oilstained earth into which my face was pressed so hard. I was agonizingly certain that the enemy, who were only a few feet away, could hear the thumping of my heart, with each loud beat chasing its predecessor at high speed. I was in the grip of terror. I began to berate myself, silently and earnestly, for my foolishness in placing my life at risk for a few grains of rice. I muttered repetitive prayers and, just as I had finished, the voices of the soldiers began to fade into the night. My sigh of relief was mixed with those of my companions as we scrambled out from under the tarpaulin.

'Bastards!' Dempsey's relief was obvious. 'Thought we were a gonner there, Johnny Mac, thought the wee bastards had us by the short and curlies, so ah did.' He wiped the beads of sweat from his brow.

Trumpeter was letting his pent-up breath escape from his lungs, now that the danger had passed. 'Bliddy Hell! Bliddy Hell! Bliddy Hell! . . . Ah thocht ah wis gonnae be sounding the Last Post for the last time . . . an that's a bliddy fact!'

I was glad to be able to make my own contribution of thankfulness for being still alive and kicking. It had been a narrow shave indeed and now was the time to count our blessings and get the hell out of here, as fast as possible, before the Japs returned. We couldn't be lucky twice in one day.

The patrol was well away now and we lost no time in descending into the inky depths of the big gun pit, filling our drum and climbing back up the iron rungs of the ladder. Dempsey, again, carried the heavy ten-gallon drum on his shoulder while Trumpeter again pulled desperately on the rope at the top. We all took a hand

56

at cursing and swearing quietly at the effort involved in trying to prevent the metal drum from clanging against the iron rungs of the ladder.

Up at the surface again at last, we rested momentarily, panting heavily from our efforts and refreshing ourselves with the cool night air. With a feeling of triumph at the near completion of our foray, we headed with all the speed we could muster back to the safety of the other side of the barbed wire once more.

We stumbled and staggered our way back between the lines, sprawling full-length, now and again, as a toe caught a stone or the raised edge of a sleeper. We had no wish to become target practice for the Jap patrol with their British-made Lee-Enfield rifles. The Gods were with us once again on this dark night and we reached the fence without serious mishap. We soon slid under it and reached the safety of our hut.

We had gambled for a second time and succeeded in outwitting our enemies. We were in solid agreement that there would be no third time. We shared the feeling that it could be third time unlucky.

But we had succeeded in our mission to provide food for four hungry mouths. Our deal with the cooks was still intact; oil for rice. We congratulated each other in the darkness of the billet lest we wake the others and looked forward to our mess-tin of 'leggy' rice in the morning, to be split four ways.

Perhaps that little, extra ration of grains of boiled rice would prove to be the extra nourishment, which enabled us to sustain ourselves and get out of the mess, we were in. Who knows? On the other hand, perhaps, the rice I had spurned when Dusty and myself were guests of the Owens sisters in Capetown would have the opposite effect.

We had survived army cooking; 'Spotted Dick' which would have needed a block and tackle to lift it from the boiler. Our stomachs had managed to digest that. If our own cooks couldn't kill us what chance did the Japs have?

Taffy was billetted in a hut further down the camp. When I saw him, I always noted the after-effects of that bashing he had received on the beach burial party. It had left a considerable mark on him. He was no longer the boisterous boyo from mid-Wales. He was very quiet and morose, brooding endlessly and seeming to inhabit a different world from the others around him. I did not see Dusty Miller now at all. He had departed on a work-party to somewhere unknown to us. I had not even known he was going until he had gone. But then, neither had he.

That was the way the Japs worked. No warning was given. They appeared from out of the blue, took whatever men they wanted and off they would go to pastures new. The move was preceded by an announcement to those concerned that they were to be moved to a 'new campo' where they would do light work and have better food. This was the carrot dangled in front of the unwary prisoners. They would be jubilant at the prospect of leaving dreadful Changi behind because 'the grass is always greener . . .' (or so they say). We were all to discover, to our dismay, that it was a worthless carrot. We were certain then that nothing could be worse than Changi and the continual hunger and monotony of the place.

I was glad when a party of Japanese officers and guards arrived at the camp and I was included in a work party of about two-hundred or so. Within half an hour we were hustled aboard army trucks, with surly looking Jap guards with rifles at the ready. We were taken to Singapore City where we were billeted at 'The Great World', a former pleasure arena, with the bare ground to sleep on. We were to be there about two months in the company of the mean-minded guards, who lost no opportunity for letting us know who was master and who was slave. Their fists, boots and rifle butts were to the fore in this operation. It made me almost wish for dear old Changi!

Each day after being paraded and split into work parties, we marched to our place of toil and shock-waves surged through us as we saw further examples of the barbarity of the Japanese. Along the route long bamboo poles had been placed and, swaying gruesomely in the wind, were the severed heads of Chinese men. They had been decapitated by their brutal conquerors and were shown for the attention of all. I shuddered and resolved to watch my step lest I keep company with these poor, savaged civilians.

I had left home as a country-boy, innocent of the ways of the big, wide world. I was fast accumulating a wealth of experience of good and evil and of the incredible bestiality of man. King George's twelve pence had bought for me the level of experience that had come to the greatest explorers and travellers in history. I had no straw sticking from my ears now.

I had travelled the world, or a considerable part of it. I had seen the good and bad of Capetown, the terrible grinding poverty of India and its system of Caste. I had had my own catastrophic involvement in the bloody battles in Malaya and the disaster of Singapore but here and now, right before my astonished eyes, was the proof of the cold, pitiless brutality of which man is capable towards his fellow man, those repulsive, bloodstained heads on slender lengths of bamboo, nodding sightless eyes towards me in the gentle wind. As for me, a prisoner, I had to stumble on through the winding roads of the rest of my life.

There were occasional rays of light in the darkness which lighted our dreary lives during those early days. We shared a road squad with some Australians. Australians are often rough and ready, often uncouth – my kind of people. They are typically good-hearted and good muckers in time of trouble and strife. They also have a ready, earthy wit.

A young Aussie had been placed in charge of the road roller. He received three gallons of petrol per day while the Jap overseer appeared unaware that the roller was fuelled with coal or wood. Some daring natives received petrol bargains while our squad received food and cigarettes in exchange.

Another task had us unloading a battered old tramp steamer at the docks and storing the cargo in a nearby godown. (warehouse) As we sweated in and out of the rat-infested holds we came across a crate, identified by its label as EX-LAX. This was, of course, a chocolate-coated purgative popular with the Western world's constipated citizens. The Japanese guards were ever on the search for plunder and one sentry enquired what the label said.

John Dempsey Kane was equal to that challenge. He informed the guard, with much signing, 'yum-yumming', and rubbing of his stomach that it was chocolate and further that it was 'Joto-taksan joto' (good – very good). The rest of the squad were enjoying JDK's deception, in a furtive manner, and it appeared that the Jap sentry did so too. He burst the crate open with his bayonet, stuffed his pockets with the goodies and closed and sealed it tightly again ensuring that the POWS would be unable to share in the spoils. With diarrhoea our constant companion, these days, it was the very last thing we needed. Like 'Little Audrey' we laughed and laughed and laughed at the thought of having attacked the enemy from the rear!

We continued with the unloading but kept an eye on the guard who was now sharing his 'chocolate' with his mates. It was difficult not to show our amusement as they pulled little squares of chocolate 'shit shatterers' (as we called them) from their pockets and stuffed them into their mouths. We hoped to be well away when the Jap realized that he had been caught 'with his trousers down,' so to speak. Meanwhile, and before the laxative began to have its effect, they licked their lips with obvious satisfaction at the delicate flavour.

We, too, were inveterate plunderers. We secreted our own plunder about our persons. There were sewing machine needles, bobbins of cotton thread made by Coats of Paisley and bicycle chains. We were accompanied back to The Great World by two older Japanese occupational troop guards. These two, whom we referred to as Tojo and Mr Moto, would go through the motions of searching us for stolen goods, but only that. They must have realized that we would try to conceal things on our persons but never once took us to task. They were reasonable and tolerant people.

This was a great bonus. We would watch nearby squads being searched methodically and then watch the beatings that followed. Mr Tojo and Mr Moto, in the course of their duties, would feel a packet of thread clenched in the hollow of our armpits and remark, with mock seriousness, 'Very bad lumpo, there. You see doctor about lumpo'. They would bend and touch a bicycle chain, sagging out of an inadequate stocking and say 'Varicose veins, very bad, dammi–dammi. No okay'. And, with affected concern, they would be on their way with a parting shot of '*Dammi Dammi. No okay!*'.

During the whole of my captivity these were to prove the only two Japanese who showed any consideration. On our way back from the docks, they also turned a blind eye on those daring Malays and Chinese who would dart amongst us to exchange small weevil-filled loaves for our merchandise. In this way we were able to acquire assorted forms of basic foodstuffs which may have proved vital in the long run. In any case, I give credit to Tojo and Mr Moto for their generous contribution to my well-being today. God bless the only two Japanese that I never titled with the word 'Bastard'.

Time and toil went by and we were suddenly returned to Changi once again. We were back to a minimal food ration with no chance of supplementing our few grains of rice with the stale, insect-infested bread to which we had become so attached.

The Japanese wanted us all to sign a paper promising not to attempt an escape. Our CO refused, quoting the Rules of War to them. His Japanese counterparts ranted and raved and punished us by herding us all into Selerang Barracks. This was an example of deliberate and unnecessary overcrowding as an act of policy to bring pressure on our leaders. The barracks had housed a battalion of Gordon Highlanders before the war and seemed ready, now, to burst at the seams with around 20,000 POWs. We were surrounded not only by squads of Japanese soldiers but also by Sikh deserters who had joined the Indian National Army, a force raised by the Japanese from the thousands of Indian prisoners they had taken. These Sikhs manned heavy machine-guns and were more than ready and well-prepared to shoot anyone who attempted to escape.

Sanitation was now again the top priority. Latrines were dug in the former drill square, with squads digging day and night to keep pace with the fierce demand. No medical supplies, whatever, were available to treat those suffering from dysentry or diarrhoea and the future dimmed.

No-one was spared the necessary digging duty. Dempsey, Trumpeter and I were awoken during the night and assigned to latrine digging. The previous squad had completed the hard work of breaking through the tar and concrete of the quadrangle and the trench was, by now, around six feet deep. As we dug further down, the urine and other human waste began to seep through the thin wall of clay separating our trench from the adjacent one and the smell became overpowering. We continued to dig and soon our feet were squelching in the, now stinking, muddied clay as we swore and sweated. We heaved a massive sigh of relief when Sergeant Joe shouted down to let us know that our spell was over for the time being, at least. We clambered out and took in great lungfuls of the relatively clean air at ground level.

Three days of this emergency passed. The Japanese had executed four prisoners trying to escape from these appalling conditions and were threatening to bring more sick and wounded troops into the barracks. Under duress, our leaders were forced to accept the demands of the enemy. We were transferred back to the original compound.

The regular commandeering of work parties continued. Not long after we had returned from the hell-hole at Selerang a thousand of us were selected for one – though we little guessed what would now befall us. I was included, as were Dempsey, Trumpeter and our old friend Taffy. Taffy was still in distress, mentally, from the bashing he had had so I was glad he was with us.

The Japanese Officer gave us the standard patter about a 'Better Campo' where we would get 'better food' and 'do light work'. Having heard those words so often before, it is, perhaps, surprising that we accepted them, choosing to believe that anywhere might be better than the hungry, dangerous situation here at Changi. 'Any where,' we thought, 'and the sooner the better'.

That same day we boarded trucks with our few belongings and bumped along the coast road which led to Singapore City.

We arrived at Singapore's Dockland and the truth then became obvious, as we were hustled off the trucks and lined up on the quay-side. After counting us several times, as was their wont, to make sure that we were all present and correct, we were made to strip naked and hurried aboard an old tramp steamer. There we endured the scalding discomfort of a quick dip in a huge tank of disinfected hot water. This done, we were sent back to the quayside, where we quickly donned our well-worn shirts, shorts, stockings and boots, while guards poked and prodded us with rifles and fists. Still soaking wet from our disinfecting, we were marched further along the docks and halted beside an even older and even rustier freighter. As I gazed at it, a memory re-awakened and an ominous familiarity dawned. Dempsey was by my side and I heard him also gasp in disbelief. This was none other than the battered old rust bucket we had unloaded a few weeks earlier, when we had enjoyed Dempsey curing the constipation of our guards.

Surely the bastards were not thinking of transporting all of us on this old tub, the *England Maru*? I could see the faded paint peeling off the thick rust on her metal plates. Surely not this stinking, rat-infested, disreputable hulk, which insulted even the lowly status of its former occupants, the cattle of the Orient? It was a reminder that our Japanese captors regarded us as less than human and in a similar category, indeed, to those cattle.

4

The *England Maru* and the Road to Hell

It seemed that this potential mass coffin was to be our mode of travel. 1,000 of us were herded into the *England Maru* and bullied down into the murky depths of the old freighter, where the excrement of its previous occupants still fouled the floor. 250 of us were crammed into each of the four holds, with only one small electric bulb stuck in a socket overhead to try to pierce the dank, darkness of our rusting metal enclosure.

The Yanks, if they saw it, would not heed to sink it. They would save their ammunition. The *England Maru* would surely sink beneath the waves on her own, for she did not seem at all seaworthy to me.

Darkness had fallen by the time the ill-tempered Japanese guards had finished mucking us about in the filthy hold. Since our last meal had been back at Changi, a half-hearted cheer arose when two wooden buckets of boiled rice were lowered down into the hold by way of ropes tied to the handles.

Confusion followed, as lack of space forebade orderly queues. With much jostling and swearing, hungry soldiers swarmed towards the lads who were dishing out the insipid and meagre, but much needed, rice ration.

Sleep was now a major priority for us all but, in the cramped conditions of that ancient ship, uninterrupted sleep was a rarity. Every now and then someone, afflicted with diarrhoea, would require the use of one of the two smelly toilet buckets. Much cursing would follow, as bodies were trampled upon during the hurried crossing to the place they were located. Even worse, there were occasions when the victim would not make it to the bucket and some unfortunate would find himself the recipient of an unwelcome gift. Stand-up fights were avoided largely due to the lack of enough room to make such fights possible.

Dempsey, Trumpeter, Taffy and I had managed to keep together. We fared a little better than most, inasmuch as we could protect the vacated space when one of us had to go to the buckets. Many of those so stricken would return during the night to find that the twelve inches of floor space they had been occupying had gone. Much frustrated effing and blinding would rent the humid air as they returned from their erratic ramblings across the minefield of packed humanity on the floor of the hold. This usually left them standing until they saw someone else rally to the call of nature and they could move in and seize the much sought-after place. The situation resembled a game of chess, with move and counter-move aimed at retaining control of the available space.

This set the tone of the next two and one half weeks. We had to contend with the ever-present outbreaks of bowel disorders and the threat of other debasing and life threatening illnesses. The sanitary arrangements were so utterly primitive that disease never seemed far away. Rats, too, scuttled across the floor of the hold or more accurately across the carpet of bodies which was packed on that floor. Mercifully, the Gods limited our fatalities to three during the crossing of the choppy South China Sea. Strangely, no physical cause was established for those three deaths. We buried them at sea and they were thrown overboard with the minimum of ceremony. A few hurried words by the Padre were allowed and even these were accompanied by the constant *Hakko! Hakko! Speedo! Speedo!* from the Japanese guards, ever callous and brutish.

It had been an inglorious end to three young lives, given in the service of their country. They were far from home but far also from the respect they should have been accorded. So much for the futility of war and all it entails; the hardships, the sacrifices and the waste of lives, both young and old. There were rewards for the victors but what of the vanquished? For them were memories of suffering, mutilated flesh and minds, and cries for help amidst blood and tears with the absence of any recognizable form of compassion.

Survival is an imperative that makes us forget all else and embrace the law of the jungle. We kill and destroy without conscience when we feel we have to. That is the grim reality. 'All is fair in love and war.'

Sanitation began to loom as a major preoccupation aboard that ship. After a night locked up with the obnoxious buckets, we would climb the metal ladder at dawn to join the endless queues on deck which waited impatiently to use an even more weird latrine which hung over the side of the ship. This unimaginable construction consisted of two planks in parallel with a space between and a shaky handrail to hold on to. It was an unstable and unreliable way of preventing an unexpected dive into the turbulent salt water below. Amidst the danger was a bonus. The seething and relentless pounding of the waves against the ship produced an ice-cold spray which performed a cleansing function hitherto neglected because of the absence of 'bumf.'

We called that lash-up 'the Stage' since our appearance on it caused endless laughter to the scores of Japanese soldiers, also in transit, who gathered to watch. They enjoyed our discomfiture as the ship pitched, yawed and dipped while we hung on for dear life to the slippery, wet and fouled planks. All this entertainment was performed with our bare bottoms exposed to the mad Japanese.

The sea water, as well as cleansing, had the effect of acting as a medication for other prevalent skin conditions. It helped ringworm, sweat rashes and our old friend from India 'dhobi's itch'. It was useful too in treating those unmentionable parasites, crabs and the large, hairy and transparent body lice which sucked at the unwashed flesh of our groins and armpits and grew fat on the blood that we could ill afford to lose. Many obnoxious predators were kept at bay by the seawater. Again I had found a touch of silver in the lining of a cloud. But the *England Maru* was a very dark cloud indeed.

The sun even seemed to shine a little for us, as the Trumpeter returned from a visit to the Stage and told Dempsey, Taffy and myself of a deal he had made with a Japanese soldier. He could swap a pair of woollen socks for a packet of Virginia cigarettes. The cigarettes were promised to be 'Englando' tobacco and not pungent, oily, cheap Malayan cigarettes but were offered in exchange for 'good woollen socks.'

66

Our wily regimental trumpeter produced from his kit a pair of socks with holes in the heels large enough to put your fist in. He folded them so that the holes could not be seen, smiled with anticipated pleasure and said, 'By the time the wee bastard finds oot, ah'll be back doon here – and we'll smoke his wee health!' With this foul statement of his intent to deceive, he was gone, up the ladder of the hold, to dishonour his bargain with the unsuspecting Japanese soldier.

Well, as Rabbie Burns proclaimed, 'The best laid plans o' mice and men gang aft agley'. Our mate returned with a victorious smile and a packet of Players Virginia fags. They had beaten us in battle but today he had evened up the score just a little. He had put one over on the enemy and it was good for a laugh as the Jap would not dare make a fuss. He would be punished for even talking to Arthur. And so we laughed our cruel, dishonest laughs as we visualized the dismay on the soldier's face when he saw the holes in the heels.

But we laughed even more when the Trumpeter opened the packet he held in his hand. We laughed, this time, at the dismay and disbelief on his face. The Japanese soldier had offloaded twenty oily, black Malayan Cigarettes in a Players packet! It was a scoring draw 'Wan each'. We saw the funny side of it and wondered if the Jap saw it too. That we would never find out, because on the next day, land was sighted and we docked at Keelung on the island of Formosa, Taiwan as it is now. We were hustled off the ship, glad, indeed, to feel the earth underneath our feet again and elated to be out of that awful, claustrophobic, rat-infested hold. I now knew what misery was suffered by caged animals. I had been one.

★   ★   ★

We were a raggle taggle bunch on that miserable, wet afternoon in November, 1942, standing in ragged columns of tired wrecks as we assembled at the dockside. Some of the men could barely stand after the ordeal of the old freighter, but those who went down were kicked brutally by the guards until they rose again. We were quickly divided into two groups of about 500 men, the groups being assigned to different camps.

I stood shivering in the cold downpour with the rain running down my face and my thin, threadbare shirt sticking to my weary body. I wondered what terrible wrong I had done to deserve the barbarous treatment I had experienced. I felt as if I was in a bottomless pit, from which I might never emerge, and that I had been abandoned by the Powers in my life, both earthly and heavenly. I prayed a silent prayer for release from my despair.

I was jerked from my melancholy as we marched from the docks and through the town of Keelung. Some of our number who were ill were assisted by others who were little better. This time we stumbled onwards without the stirring strains of 'Colonel Bogey' – this was not Capetown and the citizens were *not* applauding.

The pavements were thronged with the citizens of this northerly Formosan town. All were wearing dark coloured, shabby clothing. Every one of them, every man, woman and child, waved the Japanese flag (the 'fried egg' as we called it) but without much enthusiasm. They gazed at us with dull interest. It seemed that their military masters had dampened their spirits too. They were present, not because they wanted to be there, but because they had to.

I wondered what thoughts these impassive oriental faces concealed as they stared at the first Westerners that most of them had ever seen. How did they feel about the bedraggled, miserable state we were in? There was neither a show of pity in their sullen eyes nor any sign of pleasure at our plight. No salt was rubbed by them into the physical and mental wounds which now burdened us, as our defeat in battle was paraded before them. At least we were spared that humiliation.

With hearts as heavy as the depressing Formosan rain clouds, we made our way along the crowded streets to a railway siding. There a steam engine and some carriages awaited us and we were bullied and pressed inside by our loud-mouthed, snarling guards who helped us in with rifle-butt and boot as they screamed the inevitable '*Speedo-Speedo! Hakko-Hakko*'.

There were no cushioned seats on this train, just hard wooden benches like the old Indian trains we had used. Nevertheless, in our weary state they were a God-send upon which to rest our tired bones. No plush divan was necessary, just the rough caress of the wooden seats on my exhausted body was bliss as I sank down upon them.

★   ★   ★

We talked little since we were so fagged out. I shut my eyes and thanked my Maker for this merciful interlude and for the fresh air and solid ground all around me. I was grateful, too, that the threat was gone of being sunk by a prowling American submarine. I was away, moreover, from the humiliation of 'the Stage' and its slippery, messy planks and from the contemptible grins of the Japanese at our discomfort. It pained me to remember those howls of laughter when an occasional big wave would pound the rusty plates of the *England Maru* . . . and pound our bare arses too.

Of one thing I was certain. Nothing could ever be as bad as the ordeal on that clapped out old tramp steamer. The infamous Black Hole of Calcutta could not have been worse than the filthy, infested, claustrophobic death-cell on the *England Maru*. It had been packed to capacity with POWs, as it once had been with cattle, with two-inch long cockroaches and giant, voracious, blue bottles continually buzzing. They had seemed to be attracted to the stale sweat on our lice-infested bodies. Attracted too had been the rats that crept among us fearlessly during the dark watches of the night. They would nibble at an unprotected ear or nose. Many nights were disturbed as soldiers awakened with screams of terrified anger, causing the assailants to take flight among the soldiers of the King and to leave a trail of chaos in their passing.

The bloody cheek of such vermin. To have no regard for the soldiers of Great Britain, the soldiers who had exchanged their hearts and souls for twelve pence and the glory of an honourable field of battle.

So where was the glory we sought? Defeat and dishonour was what we had bought. Our shilling bet, invested at 'straight win', was gone forever and the end of the road loomed up menacingly in the immediate future for us all.

But still . . . things could only get better. I had already survived the worst. The future could only be better in our new camp. I actually looked forward to the redemption it had to offer. Time would tell but, for now, with delusions of luxurious living ahead, and the rhythmic clacking of the train wheels, I fell asleep.

I awoke with Dempsey's elbow in my ribs and Dempsey urging me to get off the train before some deranged Jap kicked me off. I tumbled, still half asleep, from the carriage and lined up beside the soldiers already there. We were at the far end of the line. The terminus was in a small hamlet of maybe half-a-dozen drab wooden buildings. The inhabitants were gathered nearby, watching with the same apathy as had been shown by the people in Keelung. These, down-at-heel-looking citizens wore the same colourless apparel of cheap cotton material as the people of Keelung.

It was Keelung all over again. No sympathy for our plight could be detected on the faces of these miserable-looking Taiwanese but neither did they gloat over the sight of a vanquished enemy. At least we were spared that half-expected humiliation. True to form, the blustering, abusive guards counted us again and again before bellowing 'Kiosky' at us to come to attention. Having achieved this, we were marched to a rough stony track that led away from the hamlet and made a tortuous climb into the rugged hills in the distance, where it disappeared.

My visions of better times began to look like delusions of grandeur as our escorts went out of their way to excel each other in human bestiality. They harried and bullied us at every step along the path, making no allowances for the fact that the jagged edges of granite-like rock had pierced the worn leather of many boots and feet that had become almost unbearably lacerated.

The rain, which fell incessantly, made the situation worse by getting inside our boots and causing blistering. Most of us were limping badly before we had gone very far along that road. But the guards lashed out at anyone who tarried, calling out their traditional cry of 'Speedo! Speedo! Hakko! Hakko!'. Under this tyranny we had to draw deeply upon our reserves of willpower and force ourselves on, with every yard seeming to represent a mile.

Unfortunates who were suffering from diarrhoea and had to relieve themselves by the wayside were shown no compassion. They would be at the receiving end of a hob-nailed boot or a rifle butt as they squatted in misery. Many a poor soldier was made to begin to move again before he had completed the outpouring and had to walk, stumbling, along the ever-climbing path, fouling himself as he went.

We had no option but to suffer. The guards refused us rest and some of the lads, physically exhausted, had to discard kit-bags and valises containing deeply personal and irreplaceable belongings because they could no longer bear the weight. All my own worldly possessions had been lost at Yong Peng, during my battle days in Malaya, so I had nothing to lose. In truth I was still glad of that, for I was finding the going quite tough enough with my blistered feet and I had only the togs I stood in.

What a bloody state for human beings to get into; especially proud soldiers such as we; by our own assessment, the flower of the British Army, the élite 155th (Lanarkshire Yeomanry) Field Regiment. God almighty! What would those belligerent fellows back at the siding in Lanark say if they could see us now. 'Hope the bliddy Jerries get yese!' That was their wish for us as they sought revenge for the harm some of our men had done to them. Well they had gotten their wish with an added bonus. It was the Japs that had got us, so perhaps our aggrieved friends would consider themselves fully repaid for our sins in their midst.

How I wished I was back among them, the dear people of Lanark, for they had tolerated our wrongs and had been good to us many times.

These were the jumbled thoughts that occupied my mind as I struggled up that purgatorial path that was my penance for the sin of volunteering for the Army, in response to a cry for help from my country. It was the thoughts of past 'normal' times that helped to get me through the turmoil of the present.

Even the weather was merciless and unrelenting, as the like-minded guards drove us ever upward with punishment, at each step, from rifle butt, boot and clenched fist for anyone who dared to falter. Rabbie Burns wrote that 'Man tae man the world ower will brithers be for a' that'. Well these Japanese bastards would never be 'brithers' of mine.

At last the 'breast o' the brae' was reached and our aggressive escorts ordered us to 'Yasume'. We dropped where we were. We were completely buggered with exhaustion, fatigue and pain. My heart pounded and my over-stretched lungs laboured for air after the forced march of several hours duration. It was a welcome relief to sprawl on the ground, unmindful of the cold that seeped into my sweat and rain-soaked body. I lay cursing the guards and resting my feet. The guards slaked their thirst from their water bottles with no thought for our desperate needs. 'Bastards', I thought.

Some of our fellows began to take off their boots to ease the pain of their wounded feet but an officer intervened in time with a warning of the pain that would ensue when they had to be put back on

71

again. His good advice was heeded and the easing of the pain was postponed to another time. Some of the men, including some well known 'hard men', were tearful at the pain of it all. It was an embarrassing sight.

Dempsey was nursing a foot through the rain-soaked leather. He massaged it gently but must have squeezed it too hard at one point because he gave vent to his pain, exclaiming, 'Bastard! Effin bastard' and a nearby guard identified himself with the derogatory label. (As it happened, quite correctly, since the name would have suited him quite well). He promptly clobbered John Dempsey Kane with the brass butt of his rifle, screaming '*Nanika? Dosta? Bastardo dammi-dammi. Bagerro*'. He stormed off uttering strange expletives in best Nippon-go, scowling darkly at my shattered mucker. Dempsey's lowered brows boded terrible retribution for the Jap if the opportunity presented itself in the future.

After a fifteen minute break, we were back on our feet again. I was thankful that it was downhill now and hoped fervently that the end of the road was the cluster of buildings I could see in the far distance. Every step of the way was now profound agony. Two hours later, just as it grew dark, we hobbled, limped and staggered into a village of sorts. Here we were brought to a halt in an enclosure.

It seemed that the entire population of the village that surrounded us was on parade to see us, as we shivered in the cold downpour, bedraggled and tired from our four hour long forced march. The guards shouted again and again, pushing us roughly into line to be counted. Perhaps they were concerned that one or more of us had been left dying or dead by the roadside back in the hills. They punched and prodded each man with sadistic emphasis as they satisfied themselves that everyone was present and correct. An avalanche of '*Bagerros*' and '*Dammi-Dammis*' shattered the night air. Belligerent '*Yasume Nais*' were shouted at soldiers who had been too ill or too fatigued to remain standing and had slumped into a sitting position on the wet ground. Each was savagely kicked to his feet again by some callous guard.

I noticed, as this barbarous scene was played out, that in the faces of the silent onlookers there was compassion for us. These people, like the residents of Keelung, had their 'Fried egg' flags, but were not waving them. I sensed a kindred spirit close at hand. It seemed, as they stared at us with eyes that showed no pleasure in our deplorable condition, that there was an almost telepathic communication of their distaste for the domineering, repulsive Japanese.

Two Japanese officers now appeared and, after they had conversed briefly with the guards, we were on our way once more. We made our way painfully down a short hill and thence upwards on the opposite hillside to where I could see a collection of huts surrounded by a high bamboo fence.

At last we came to the open gates of what I guessed was to be our new camp, and entered a large square of open ground opposite some huts. Here we were halted. We were glad that our destination had at last been reached. Through the window of the nearest hut I could see long raised platforms throughout its length on each side. Upon these platforms, at regular intervals, bundles were placed. These comprised two blankets folded neatly and a small, circular pillow. A great relief swept over me, as I realized that the better times I had predicted had come to pass. I was looking forward to wrapping the blankets around my protesting body and enjoying a much-needed sleep.

The endless discomfort, humiliation and pain of recent weeks had been a terrible ordeal but a silver lining was emerging from the black cloud at last. We had reached our Eden. The 'England Maru' was behind us, as was Changi; so too was the forced march. The new camp would recompense us. I thanked God and Our Lady for delivering me from evil – but I put in a word for Buddha, Mohammed and Krishna too – just in case they, too, had a hand in it. I was willing to thank them all.

Little did I know that at this black hill, this place of utter desolation among the dark, forbidding mountains, we had in fact reached our Calvary. We would be crucified, not on the hill but deep inside its bowels. This 'paradise' would claim the lives of many of my companions and my 'silver lining' would be shown to be a mirage, a product of my wishful thinking.

It is as well that our Maker does not permit us to know what the future holds for us. For this gift we should be truly thankful. The Lord is our Shepherd as the Psalmist says. But His flock is scattered on various roads, some smooth and easy to traverse, some rugged, and sore to the traveller. We, who had received the hard end of the shepherd's crook, wondered at His ways at times, often wondering, 'Why me? For what sin am I being punished?'

But Life is what it is and we must accept our burden, small or large, and make the best of it. Or we must perish by the wayside.

Why Lord?

Why, Lord, hast thou forsaken me?
As thou once were by foul decree;
When dark deeds at Gethsemane
Betrayed thee to the enemy.

Why am I here in this foul place?
This hell on earth – Nippon's disgrace.
Humiliated, Tojo's lackey;
A coolie here, in Kinkasaki.

Beaten, starved, just skin and bone;
Degraded, humbled, spirit gone.
Bereft of dignity and cowed;
A zombie – once so brave and proud.

What sin, dear Lord, did I commit?
I volunteered to do my bit,
And do my bit I did, I swear,
And my reward? This yoke I bear.

Not even thirty shekels paid
For my life Lord, for I'm afraid
Compared to thee I am but naught,
Abandoned here to bloody rot.

Why, Lord, hast thou forsaken me,
When just this once I needed thee?

5

Kinkasaki

I knuckled my brow and thanked the Almighty for my good fortune. The hard days of Changi and the harder days of the *England Maru* were well behind me now, not forgetting the hellish forced march up the rocky mountainside. Soon, I hoped, I would be given a meal of sorts and some water to ease my poor, parched throat. Then I could attend to the painful blisters on my swollen, bleeding feet. Foolish thoughts in my desperate quest for succour and salvation from adversity. All too often we discover that dreams have no real substance. Our awakening becomes as a bubble bursting and drenching us with reality.

My fanciful dreamings of the alleviation of my present distressful state were brought to an abrupt end by the butt of a rifle thudding into the small of my back and a maniacal guard screaming, '*Kioski! Kioski!*' I sprang to attention with the rest of my exhausted comrades and so prevented further brutal abuse by the snarling guard. I now experienced a real doubt as to my 'betterment' at this dark and isolated new camp. Time would surely tell whether fate had dealt a plus or a minus; an ace or a deuce.

Dempsey, who was by my side, muttered, 'Some day I'll shove that bastard's rifle where he'll feel it most – butt first', and I sincerely hoped that he would get his wish and that I'd have a rifle too. Perchance to dream.

Two Japanese officers appeared now, atop a nearby platform, with a couple of NCOs in attendance and stood looking down on our dishevelled, rainsodden, pathetic ranks with open contempt on their cold and stern faces. One of them – a dead ringer for Napoleon Bonaparte – began to address us in a haughty manner, informing us that he was the Camp Commandant and that he welcomed us to Kinkasaki's copper mine. Each word uttered was like ice from the Arctic and his oriental, almond eyes were of a similar, contemptuous coldness. He informed us that if we worked hard in the copper mine we would get food to eat. If we did not work hard, then we would get *no* rice. This chilling information from the small, haughty figure who confronted us did nothing to console us in our present state of mental and physical dejection. I could now see a big, black cloud hovering above us.

So we stood shivering under the watchful eyes of the sullen guards with the ominous message ringing in our ears; Kinkasaki was not going to be a holiday camp. I was beginning to wish that I was back with the hardships at Changi. The illusion that the grass is greener on the other side of the fence was clearly false. Each move to the next rung of the ladder was a step to the rung below. We live and we learn! I had qualified for 'The key of the door' at the Battle of Slim River. I now began to wonder if I would see the age of twenty-two.

The '*Bunsho Dono*', as we would come to know Wakiyama, the Camp Commandant, stood resplendent in his neat, made to measure uniform with highly polished jack boots and white gloved hand on the hilt of his samurai sword. He gazed down on this group of 525 despondent POWs, completely unmindful of their sodden shirts and shorts and of the bloodied water oozing from their saturated boots. Through the faltering efforts of a little, fat interpreter, he continued with his message of impending doom,

'You men . . . you all disgrace to country. You surrender in battle. Nippon soldier not surrender. He not lay down arm. Japanese soldier brave soldier. Japanese soldier die for Emperor of Japan. All time England say Nippon coolie. Now *you* coolie; and will *work* like coolie in copper mine. And if you not work hard like coolie in mine . . . you will be *punish hard* like coolie.'

And with that final, dismal threat, he turned on his heel and was gone, leaving us chilled by his tyrannical tirade and concerned about our future here at Kinkasaki and the unknown harshness of its copper mine.

With the departure of Wakiyama, the guards came to life again, and all was a frenzy of activity. Instead of being allowed into the sanctuary of the huts, we were herded into a nearby building, stripped naked and our boots and tattered clothing taken away. We were issued with old, but clean, second hand army trousers and jackets and a pair of roughly foot shaped flat pieces of wood with a thick canvas strap across the front to wear on our feet. The issue of rough – but welcome – clothing complete, we were fingerprinted and given a number (mine was 325). Only when this was finished were we divided into groups of around thirty and permitted to enter the huts allotted to us. Dempsey, Trumpeter, Taffy and I were part of Number 2 Squad and it was with great relief that we entered our hut and escaped the scrutiny of the guards for the moment. We viewed our new digs with mixed feelings. We had been promised 'better camps'. Time would tell.

Each hut had two raised platforms with rice bag matting covering the wooden boards. Each man had two rough but cleanish army blankets and a small, cylindrical canvas pillow filled with rice husks. A clean second hand shirt of flannel-like material was also provided. This was a welcome bonus. The width of the folded blankets plus a few inches more, amounted to the width of platform which would be each man's bed for our time at Kinkasaki. This amounted to roughly twenty inches – slightly better than the *England Maru*.

Outside, long lengths of bamboo piping pierced by holes at regular intervals provided primitive washing facilities, which carried cold water to a communal washing trough. There was a steady queue at these troughs as the inmates of the huts did their best to alleviate the pain of their blistered feet with the soothing balm of the cold water from Mother Nature's bounty. The guards, some of whom were Taiwanese left us in peace for a while and then it was a return to savagery as they hustled us back into the huts and the two dim light bulbs were extinguished.

By now it was the early hours of the morning and, cursing the 'goons', as we were to christen them, we drifted into the anaesthesia of sleep and escape from our ordeal. I dreamed my dreams of yesterday, when tragedy was a boil on the neck or worse, the backside. I dreamed of my beloved Lanark and drooled over the tasteless hard tack, which our cooks had provided – burnt offerings for dinner and watery gruel at which Oliver Twist would have turned up his nose. Those much maligned morsels, now attained the status of five star cuisine in my new found circumstances as a guest of the Emperor Hirohito. My empty belly cried out for a helping of plum duff (alias Spotted Dick) and all the other food, which we had treated with disdain. I can now appreciate that the hard tack was one element of our preparation for arduous times ahead – like now, when our only sustenance was a handful of boiled rice three times a day – saltless and sugarless and never enough of it.

★   ★   ★

My dreams of the past were shattered as I felt something hard thudding into my spare ribs and I was back to grim reality once more as I looked up at the glaring guard who stood astride me. Again he sunk his heavy hobnailed boot into my side and then into my back, snarling and screaming at me to get up. '*Yasume nai. No sleepo . . . sleepo dammi, dammi. Bagerro.*'

There was confusion and chaos all around the billet as bewildered and frightened POW's received the same treatment as myself from other ill tempered goons and were on their feet and surging through the open door to the parade ground outside. With great urgency, to escape further brutality, I too leaped to my feet and joined the panic-stricken exodus from the hut, limping painfully, as were others, from the open blisters on my feet. It was still pouring with rain as we stood there – all 525 of us, bewildered at this sudden onslaught by the guards. A Japanese sergeant was roaring orders at the goons and they started to count us yet again and, satisfied that all were present and correct, we were hustled back into our huts with the usual cries of '*Speedo! Speedo! Hakko! Hakko!*' We were to experience many of these sudden check ups in the future. Once out of earshot of our brutal tormentors there was much cursing and a quick rub down with any piece of dry material which we could find. Then back between the blankets and the fervent hope that the bastards would leave us alone for a few hours rest.

At six in the morning they had us up again, but left us alone this time to don the clothes with which we had been issued, perform our ablutions and acquaint ourselves with the latrines. These were a

1. Young Yeomen. JM (aged 18) with his brother Richard (aged 22) as newly fledged Troopers in the Lanarkshire Yeomanry in 1939.

2. 'B' Troop, The Lanarkshire Yeomanry, 1939. (JM Standing third from left in the rear rank.)

3. With 'Dusty' Miller in Edinburgh, 1941.

4. The P&O liner *SS Strathmore* in which the 155th (LY) Field Regiment RA sailed from Greenock for Bombay in March, 1941. *(Photo: Hulton Getty Picture Library).*

5&6. Ahmadnagar, 1941.

Top: On the Gun Park with one of our 4.5" Howitzers. (JM right.)

Bottom: Outside our barrack room with Acha, our bearer. (JM seated left.)

7. Japanese troops mopping up in Kuala Lumpur, 11 January, 1942. *(Photo: IWM HU2770).*

8. Singapore, 15 February, 1942. The Surrender. Lieutenant Generals Percival and Yamashita Tomoyuki discussing terms. *(Photo: IWM HU2770.)*

9. 'The Changi Oil Syndicate' (left to right) John 'Dempsey' Kane and JM (in their 'demob suits', 1945) and Arthur 'Trumpeter' Smith (recent photo).

10. The 'Selerang Incident', 30 August, 1942. Over 20,000 POW were crammed into Selerang Barracks (designed for 120 men) for refusing to sign an undertaking not to escape. (Photo: IWM HU43339.)

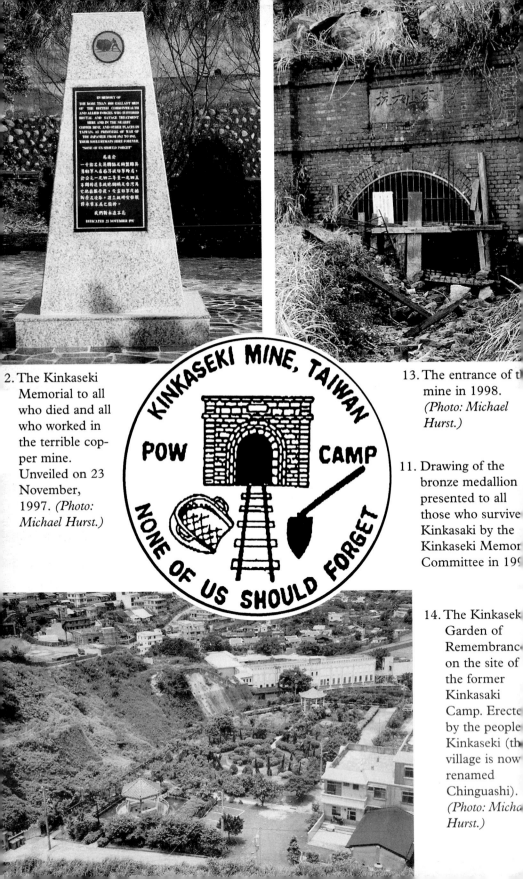

2. The Kinkaseki Memorial to all who died and all who worked in the terrible copper mine. Unveiled on 23 November, 1997. *(Photo: Michael Hurst.)*

KINKASEKI MINE, TAIWAN

POW CAMP

NONE OF US SHOULD FORGET

13. The entrance of t mine in 1998. *(Photo: Michael Hurst.)*

11. Drawing of the bronze medallion presented to all those who survive Kinkasaki by the Kinkaseki Memor Committee in 199

14. The Kinkasek Garden of Remembranc on the site of the former Kinkasaki Camp. Erecte by the people Kinkaseki (th village is now renamed Chinguashi). *(Photo: Micha Hurst.)*

15. JM with Nan, November, 1945.

16. And in October, 1998.

BUCKINGHAM PALACE

The Queen and I bid you a very warm welcome home.

Through all the great trials and sufferings which you have undergone at the hands of the Japanese, you and your comrades have been constantly in our thoughts. We know from the accounts we have already received how heavy those sufferings have been. We know also that these have been endured by you with the highest courage.

We mourn with you the deaths of so many of your gallant comrades.

With all our hearts, we hope that your return from captivity will bring you and your families a full measure of happiness, which you may long enjoy together.

George R.I

September 1945.

17. JM's copy of the letter sent by HM King George VI to all returning Far East Prisoners of War.

welcome change from the boreholes at Changi and the awful, humiliating 'Stage' on the *England Maru*. They consisted of a row of concrete-built individual toilets with a half-door for privacy and a hole in the floor. Almost luxurious compared to our previous toilet facilities – but again, as usual, there was no sign of any 'bumf'.

One night-time journey to these latrines made a particular mark on my memory. I had to go in the early hours of the morning. I didn't see one of the Taiwanese night guards, who was hiding in deep shadow in a corner. He bellowed at me to stop where I was and accused me of failing to bow to him as I passed. He immediately punched me in the face and when I protested that I had not seen him he laid into me again and then made me stand in the miserable cold drizzle that seemed always to be falling. I stood there for half an hour, drenched and miserable. By the end of this demeaning treatment, I had already responded to nature's call, on the spot where I stood shivering and silently cursing the depraved sadist. Eventually he let me go and I resolved to give this particular psycho a wide berth in future . . . if possible.

Each morning, two men from each squad were detailed to bring the rations from the cookhouse, where three or four of our own men had been roused earlier and had cooked the rice and heated the water to wash it down. This was quickly distributed among us and just as quickly eaten. We were still starving on the first morning, as the rice had been our first meal since leaving the *England Maru*. But we were getting used to being hungry by now and, however inadequate the ration, it was very welcome, with every grain assuming enormous proportions. We ate it and cursed the Japs for starving us.

The rest of the day was taken up with a superficial medical examination by a small and bespectacled Japanese NCO. He prodded us here and there and said, '*Yosh, Okayka.*' And that was that. Then we lined up at the building where we had been fingerprinted the night before and were issued with a black-painted cardboard hat, a shirt and shorts of a green coloured pack sheet material* and a pair of cloth-uppered, thin, composition rubber-soled boots and were told that

---

* Pack sheet; a rough, loosely woven material, like Hessian. Normally used for baling such merchandise as raw cotton or flax. Probably made from jute.

these were the clothes which we would wear when working in the mine.

We were then left alone to ponder our future and speculate what the copper mine would be like. One of the few older men in our midst assured us that it would be 'a piece of cake'. Fetlar, as he was known, had been a coal miner in the pits near Motherwell in Lanarkshire. A small, wiry man, he promised to 'keep us right' adding, with mature wisdom, that it would be out of the effin' rain and that it would be nice and warm down there.

Well, unfortunately, out of the mouths of babes and balloons can emerge wind and water. The Fetlar was to be proved correct in that the copper mine would be warm but just how warm it would be we were to find out the very next day in the gut and mind-sapping furnaces of the 'holes' in which we would have to toil.

We received three small bowls of boiled rice that first day and some watery vegetable soup with the last ration of rice and this was to be the standard, unvarying menu for the remainder of our internment in the camp. Whilst working in the mine, we would carry the mid-day ration with us and we were eternally hungry – with never enough to fill our empty bellies. Bedtime again and, as the guards had kept their distance all day, I thought that perhaps, there was light in the tunnel after all.

I dreamt that night once more of Lanarkshire and the beautiful Clyde Valley where I had been born and lived, and of the tasty hot pot which my mother would make at the weekend as a change from the usual tatties and mince. I dreamt also of the mouth watering 'clootie dumplings' which she would pack into a clean pillow case and cook in a large cast iron pot, kept for the cooking of this delicacy, until the hungry rumblings in my belly threatened to wake me up. I switched then to thoughts of my betrothed Nan and when I would see her again. Despite the hardness of the boards of the sleeping space I slept comfortably enough, bringing peace to my aching flesh and bones. The flannelette shirt was soft and comfortable and, I considered, things could be worse.

*　　*　　*

At six am, things started to become worse. The guards stormed into our huts, screaming and shouting at us to stand to our beds.

'Kioski! Yasume nai! No sleepo! Dammi, dammi!'

Still half asleep, we stood to attention on the floor at the foot of our bed space. Into the hut strode a mean looking Japanese sergeant and two Jap guards, who intimated to us that we had to number off. (*Tenko*) This was to be our initiation into Nippon-go and its numerary system.

We were made to number off in English and, as each of us called our number, the Japanese guard would give the Japanese equivalent: '*Ichi, nee, san, see, goh, rocco, sichi, hachi, ku, du*' and so on. Then we had to number off in Japanese again, with any mistakes being punished by a rap on the head with the stout bamboo rod held by the irate sergeant. We were made to repeat our '*bango*' session until the sergeant was satisfied that we were more or less proficient and stamped out of the hut again, leaving us to get on with our ablutions.

Breakfast followed with the usual small ration of rice with warm water to wash it down and everyone still hungry when the meal was over. Then, one of our NCOs entered the hut to inform us of the future routine which our captors would impose on us.

Each squad had to nominate a '*hancho*' (squad chief) who would be responsible for giving details of the squad to the guards at each roll call. One man volunteered for this 'promotion' and everyone gave unanimous approval and wished him 'the best of British' as no one else fancied the job.

We must bow to any Japanese soldier we came near – or suffer the consequences. He told us that we would be going down the mine that same day on an instructive visit and that we had to wear our pack sheet shirt and shorts, our cardboard mine helmet and the boots with which we had been issued.

An hour later, we were told to visit the cookhouse where we would be given food to take down the mine with us. I queued with my mates and was given an oblong wooden box measuring about seven inches by four by three. This was half full of boiled rice with a few strands of pickled seaweed on top.

We were then paraded, with our rice boxes tied to our belts with odd pieces of string, and issued with a small carbide lamp and a small piece of carbide. We then marched out of camp, accompanied by half a dozen guards. We had to climb a flight of rough rocky steps leading to the top of the hill and then down to the mine on the other side. By this time our legs were aching sorely and, in our undernourished state, we were almost exhausted. The Camp Commandant had refused to allow any of the sick men to remain in camp, with the result that many of these poor lads had to be supported by their companions during the trek. We were to find that this would be a routine occurrence as our Japanese masters strove to increase the output of copper from the mine.

We gazed around us at the huddle of mine buildings and the entanglement of narrow gauge rail tracks running into a dark tunnel cut into the mountain. Our eyes then strayed to the large, metal bogies which sat on the tracks – bogies which would become massive thorns in our flesh before very long. At the minehead stood a shinto shrine, decorated with orange blossom shrubs and with Japanese characters adorning its canopy. Here, we were ordered to halt and shout '*Kerri!*' bowing low as we did so. As we followed this order I heard Dempsey, who was by my side, mutter 'Bastards!' instead of '*Kerri!*' and I accompanied his irreverent blasphemy.

There were mining *hanchos* (gaffers) present and these now attached themselves to different squads. They wore the same black helmets as us but with one broad, white bar painted on each side and these men, we discovered later, were Taiwanese. Nearby, watching us, were other *hanchos* with two broad, white bars painted on their helmets. We came to know that these were the top gaffers down the mine and were Japanese.

The bowing and scraping finished, we moved to the mouth of the nearby tunnel and here the one bar *hancho*, who appeared to be in charge of our Number 2 Squad, showed us how to work our carbide lamps. This was done by pouring water into the hollow top and adjusting the screw which acted as a regulator. The gas accumulated and forced its way through the nozzle at the front of the lamp. He lit his own, which was an improvement on the ones we had, with its larger, well polished reflector, and lit one of ours, which in turn provided light for the others. This done, he led the way into the darkness of the wide cavern. We followed, with the light from the lamps throwing grotesque shadows on the jagged sides of the tunnel as we stumbled along. The atmosphere was eerie as we trundled along in the wake of our *hancho*, trying not to fall between the uneven planks of wood that spanned the sides of the bogie rails and had dirty, smelly water flowing underneath. A hundred yards further into the interior brought calamity to one of our men as he stood on the loose end of a plank and found himself up to his waist in a polluted drain. With true British humour, we all cheered loudly at him and hurled abuse as filthy as the water he floundered in, he, meanwhile, cursing his luck as he clambered out of the filth.

The *hancho* was well in front of me so I couldn't see whether he, too, had enjoyed the spectacle, but he very soon let us know that he was, most definitely the boss. He turned off the main tunnel into a narrow, untimbered passageway which dipped sharply down unevenly spaced steps cut out of the dull, damp, rock. Trumpeter was a few men in front of Dempsey and I and, with all of us bent almost double beneath the low roof of this offshoot passage, he started to sing the dwarfs' song from Snow White. 'Hi ho, Hi ho, it's off to work we go.' As others joined in, the *hancho* stopped in his tracks and turning, his face black as thunder, yelled, '*No sing! No sing! Dammi, dammi! No okay! Bagerro!*' and, lifting the long handled hammer that he carried, whacked the nearest chanters across the shoulders. Then, turning away with a domineering scowl, went on his way along the low, crumbling, unsupported passageway. Meanwhile, Snow White's serenaders lapsed into silence!

The cool of the main tunnel had long since been left behind. So intense was the heat becoming, that it seemed that each step down into the mine raised the temperature by one degree. The heat was at suffocating level now and sweat was literally pouring from all parts of my aching body and stinging my eyes as I stumbled further down into the incinerating depths of this hellish pit. My shirt and shorts were saturated with sweat and my feet slipped and squelched about in my shoddy footwear. What a bloody state of exhaustion and pain we were all in as we plodded along in the shadowy light of our lamps – half of which had been extinguished by acidic water dripping on them from the roof. Snow White's seven dwarfs wouldn't have been singing if they had worked here and their beards would have been well and truly singed by the awful heat.

We turned off into another narrow tunnel which proved to be a dead end. Here our *hancho* allowed us to '*yasume*' (rest) for a few minutes. With great relief, everyone sank to the ground, not caring that it was wet and filthy – we were wet and filthy ourselves anyway between sweat and the drips from the roof. We were all gasping for breath because of the lack of oxygen in this area of the mine. Morale was very low as we crouched on our hunkers and worried about what the future had in store for us. What terrible sins had we committed in our past to deserve this punishment? Was it because of our misdeeds in Lanark? No, our sin was that we had laid down our arms and surrendered to the enemy instead of fighting to the last man as Mr Churchill had wanted. Yet *we* had not surrendered. Our generals had made that decision for us but *they* would never be asked to work in the mine.

But surely the Japs wouldn't expect us to work in the conditions that we were experiencing at the moment. Surely the rules of war forbade such cruelty. But, as my mind clutched at straws, cold reason reminded me of our treatment up till now and I realized that the future looked very bleak indeed.

One of our men, Gunner Ponsonby, from Birmingham, suffered from asthma and was in the process of an attack just now. He was gasping for breath, struggling to get air into his lungs and was looking really ill. There was nothing we could do for him as there were no medical facilities, so his survival was in the lap of the gods. Soon, the scowling *hancho* had us back on our feet again and, pointing to a rickety-looking ladder which led upwards through the roof of the tunnel, intimated that we should follow him as he mounted it. One by one, we climbed the ladder, with much swearing as we slipped on the wet rungs – or worse, discovered that a rung was missing or broken. This usually resulted on a sodden, dirt caked foot thumping down on someone's head with much indignant cursing from the abused man.

What a mess we were in as we climbed up that shambles of a ladder within the claustrophobic tunnel, with acid water dripping from above and stinging our eyes and making the rungs slippery as the water mingled with the copper ore dust. With grit fouling the jets of our carbide lamps and leaving us in darkness and, with each rung negotiated, the terrible heat increasing, we finally found ourselves at the top – in a wide, low-roofed cavern where the heat was so ferocious that it left us gasping for air that was not there.

Unbelievable! I began to wonder if I had been killed in battle and this was Hell. But this was no nightmare in a dream world. This was real. This was our world now – a living hell – with a snarling *hancho* as old Nick.

Dante must have been inspired by that hellish place. He must surely have visited here for I had a vision of Hell as I stood in the searing heat, watching our grotesque shadows writhe on the walls of this awesome hole in the bowels of the earth.

A number of small flattish baskets and *chunkals* (hoe-like tools) lay nearby. The *hancho* showed us how to scoop the ore into these containers and then throw it into the chute which was situated by the side of the ladder. He watched as we copied his example and cleared the rest of the rubble. Each of us had a basket, shuffling backwards and forwards like the coolies which the Buncho Dono had said we would be. I did not like this experience of slavery. I was completely exhausted, as were all of my fellow prisoners, with each basket feeling heavier than the one before and rest denied us.

The pile of copper ore having been cleared from the floor of the 'hole', the *hancho* called a halt and we followed him back down the ladder, jostling with one another as we sought to escape the heat of the hole. We sought to take refuge in the tunnel which was a little cooler although still very hot. Another horror awaited. The *hancho* had not realized that Ponsonby had remained in the tunnel, unable to climb the ladder into the hole. As he lay on the ground, still fighting for breath, the furious *hancho* screamed, '*Bagerro. Dammi, dammi! Bioki (sick) no okay. Dammi, dammi*', all the while striking Ponsonby on the head with the long shaft of his hammer.

Dempsey tried to intervene on Ponsonby's behalf, explaining that Ponsonby was unable to breathe and found himself on the receiving end of a beating from the bastard's hammer. This was our introduction to the slavery we were to experience during the next two and a half years in this camp.

★   ★   ★

The mine was worked on several levels, with 'work holes' on each level. The POW's had to fill a set number of bogeys with the ore which they tipped into the chute of the hole in which they were working. In our early days in the mine, the Japs manipulated us. They set a number of bogeys to be filled for each hole e.g. four PoWs

87

working in a hole would have to fill eight bogeys. When this was done, they could finish for the day. So, we would get on with the job, and be finished with time to spare, which we could spend in the cooler tunnel and eat what was left of the rice in our rice boxes. (We would regularly find rats gnawing at the boxes when we returned and often find cockroaches inside the boxes when we opened them. We ate the rice nevertheless, and might well have eaten the cockroaches too, if we could have caught them).

What we did not realize was that the Japs were taking note of how quickly we were able to meet our quota. They began to add a bogey here, a bogey there, to our original requirement and, too late, we realized that sometimes we could not make our quota. When this happened, the offending squads would be lined up at the end of the day and made to hold on to the compressed air pipes which ran along the top of the passage wall. The *hancho* then whacked their buttocks and the backs of their thighs with his hammer.

Everyone suffered during these beatings – the poor unfortunates who were being beaten and were trying to stifle their sobs and those who were forced to watch their comrades suffer humiliation and pain – and yet were thankful that they themselves were not on the receiving end on this occasion. These beatings became a daily occurrence in the mine. Both Taiwanese and Japanese overseers took a sadistic satisfaction from the brutality inflicted on emaciated, demoralized British soldiers.

So it was that those beatings became an additional terror, as we slaved to fulfil our quota of bogeys to avoid that humiliation. And we felt despair as we witnessed once proud and hardy soldiers reduced to cowed, spiritless zombies, flinching from the pain of the *hancho*'s hammer and suffering the demeaning frustration of being unable to control their bowels during those beatings and soiling themselves.

★   ★   ★

As the days and weeks wore on, men began to die – from the unsupported roofs falling in; from the slavery and the hammerings; from broken rungs on ladders; from falling into uncovered chute openings; from starvation; from dysentry; from berri-berri. Then, as the death toll mounted, men began to die from sheer despair and from lack of will power – they just became unable to keep plodding on through the abject blanket of gloom which shrouded us all during our time at Kinkasaki. Every day, men would line up on sick parade, weeping and pleading with Doctor Seed to say that they were not fit to go down the mine. The doctor was distraught as he explained to them that he could not help. Even sick men had to work in the mine.

I had a brush with death during a spell as a 'bogey-man.' The chute from the work hole above had become clogged with some extra-large rocks half-way up. I had to try to free the blockage. I balanced myself precariously on the side of a bogey to reach the blockage with the long pole used for this purpose. I poked and prodded hard at the ore lodged in the chute, meanwhile holding on to the timber frame of the chute with my left hand. I was too successful. Suddenly the entire load came thundering down at me and a huge lump of ore struck a glancing blow to my bare hip-bone as I slewed myself partially away from it. I was lucky to be only bruised, although particles of grit were embedded in my right hip. Had my evasive reflex action been slower I would surely have been killed. A Taiwanese civilian worker was close by and gave me first aid. He broke open a cigarette and pressed the raw tobacco into the broken skin on my hip. It was a rough-and-ready, but effective anti-septic and ready to hand. It was then back to work. Until the end of the shift.

Back at camp, Doctor Seed was equally resourceful. He produced an old razor blade which he used to gouge out the grit which had become embedded. He worked with all the gentleness and care of which he was capable.

I had thought that Changi was bad and was glad to be away from it. And in suffering the purgatory of the *England Maru* I had wished that I had never left Changi. Nothing, I had thought, could be as bad as that rusty old ship with its rat infested holds and the sea water cascading in, soaking us as we tried to sleep, packed like livestock, on its cattle soiled floor.

And then, during the forced march to Kinkasaki, I had thought that nothing could be worse than the exhaustion, the pain, the abuse from the guards as they used rifle butts and boots to force us ever onwards and upwards to the camp. Would I never learn that the grass is not always greener somewhere else?

Fetlar, the coal miner who had promised to 'keep us right, was so shocked with the conditions on his first visit to the mine that he did his pants a mischief. He also took a piece of rock and bashed his hand and injured it quite severely. This, together with the fact that he was a fair bit older than the rest of us, meant that he was excused from any further work in the mine and did camp duties from then on. Soon afterwards, a young man from the 5th Field Regiment tried the same desperate fraud. He received a punching from the suspicious Japanese medical corporal and was back down the mine the next day, with the added misery of two self inflicted broken fingers. This failed fraud was never again attempted by anyone.

The days of mental and physical torment went on, with the barbarous guards forcing sick, incapable POWs to work in the mine. These poor men often had to be assisted up the punishing two hundred and fifty steps to the top of the hill and then down nearly nine hundred steps on the other side to reach the mine. When they reached the work-place, the devious *hanchos* would put one sick man along with two or three other men, who had to work even harder to fulfil the quota for the 'passenger' as well as themselves. The 'passenger' would sit in a corner of the hole all day, so mentally and physically fatigued from illness and the journey to the mine, that he was unable to perform any work. This tactic by the Japs meant that there were more and more hammerings each day as bogey quotas could not be met. So exhausted and gaunt and haggard were we that none escaped the fiendish wrath of the *hanchos* – including the 'passengers'. These abused, ill prisoners would have to be carried back to the camp at the end of the day, trying to hide their tragic tears of anguish and humiliation, and we would pretend not to notice their sorrowful indignity as we tried to hide our own.

Back at camp, once proud, valiant men, reduced now to servile Zombies, would join the shuffling sick queue, pleading with the doctor for some time away from the mine. But instead, 'Big Jim, a gentle English giant', and 'Geordie from Newcastle', and 'Beau Brummy' from Birmingham, and 'Scouser' and 'Taffy' and Jocks would be given charcoal or chalk powders while the heartbroken doctor explained that he was powerless to keep them from the mine. The Japs would allow only the most desperately ill to remain in camp. Despite despair and trauma, it was back down the bloody mine for the sick the next day. There was no escape and some would break down and weep at the thought of work and punishment again on the morrow. And we, who watched, would see our own reflection as in a mirror and wonder when the day would come when we would be as they, and unable to contain our own grief.

Charcoal and chalk powder was the only medicine available, with the charcoal being provided by the cooks, who used wood to cook the rice. So, we would shuffle our way along the endless sick queue and receive our medicine – black or white – and swallow it with the thought that if it didn't do us any good, then it wouldn't do us any harm. At the end of the first nine months in Kinkasaki, we were in such a dreadful state of general weakness and ill health, that the Japs brought prisoners from other camps to work in the mine. At the same time, they transferred some of the weakest in our camp to those other camps. The men to be transferred were chosen as we paraded for work in the morning. One of the Japs would point at this lucky man or that, and they would be amongst the fortunate few who would have their prayers answered and be able to leave the grim atrocities of the mine behind.

These parades were known as 'thin man' parties. Each time, we would try to look even thinner and more ill than we actually were, as we tried desperately to escape Kinkasaki by the only route available other than death. I bombarded Heaven on each and every one of these occasions with pleas and prayers for my escape but to no avail, I never did escape the dire bondage. Neither did Dempsey or Taffy. Trumpeter did though, on the very first of the clearances. Perhaps God mistook him for me! It was a lucky dip – with men left behind who were worse off than those who got away.

As though things were not bad enough already, we were beset by a plague of giant worms which infested our intestines – some as long as seven inches. They were transparent, disgusting to look at and repulsive to the touch. We could feel them travel the length of our bowels and windpipes and protrude from our anus or throat. Since no medicine was available from the Japs, our doctors had to come up with a cure themselves. They discovered that boiled seaweed was a powerful purgative. The fact that the worms disliked the brew was a bonus. Shortly after I was dosed with the 'seaweed cure', I felt a calamitous disturbance within me as the parasites reacted to the vile concoction and sought the quickest exit. I rushed to the latrines and got there just in time as my guts erupted and I felt the evil vermin on the move. The threshing parasites were ejected unceremoniously from my throat and my bottom in one mad rush, to lie writhing in their death throes in the foul depths of the latrine. We thanked God for his gift of seaweed and for our doctors and medical orderlies who had triumphed against the odds.

I contracted dysentery and got to know the terrible gut wrenching, strength-sapping pain of this wasting disease. It causes countless visits to the toilet each day and strips the lining from the stomach. A gnawing fierce ache assails you as the flesh is stripped from your bones. I don't remember being taken to the hut which served as a hospital, (in name only, as the patients lay on the same type of bare wooden platform as in the other huts). I was seriously ill and at the mercy of the Gods as our MO's still had no medical supplies whatever. Their improvised medicine for dysentery was rice water (again provided by our cooks) and I remember being fed this balming liquid by one of the medical orderlies or doctors. I was too ill and too weak even to be able to feed myself.

And then, out of the blackness shone a ray of light. A batch of Red Cross parcels arrived at the camp – the only ones which came our way – and with them a case of medical supplies. A gift from God it seemed. I remember too, that Doctor Peter Seed came to me as I lay dying in that hut and, putting a small phial to my lips, told me to drink the contents. He explained that it was liquid opium. As I drank it, I remember the most wonderful, warm glow inside me as it caressed my lacerated stomach, alleviating the soul destroying ache that was my constant companion. And I remember the look of compassion in the eyes of this gentle, gentle man as he gazed at my rickle of bones and wasted flesh. I felt that I had died in that gloomy hut of death and that the hand of God had been administered to me by way of this quiet doctor, a man only a few years older than myself. Doctor Seed was ill himself at this time and was taken from Kinkasaki, desperately sick, to another camp in March, 1945. He died only a few years after the war ended.

I recovered slowly after Dr Seed's attention and, after a week or two of camp duties, was back down the mine again, not fully fit but in keeping with the others who trudged wearily up and down the rugged hillside to our pit of penance.

I no longer complained about going down the mine now. I was philosophical about my present situation. I had been dead and was alive again by the grace of God and his mediator, Dr Seed. I counted my blessings and gave thanks to those concerned – the cooks for the rice water which they skimmed from the cooking rice; the medical orderlies who attended to my drained body; to the two MO's and last, but not least, God himself.

Afterwards, as I toiled in the depths of Kinkasaki's infamous mountain, sweating and weakening, I thought back to the time that I lay in that make-believe hospital hut and remembered the poor souls that lay dying there, some with advanced berri-berri, with testicles the size of footballs and stomachs and faces bloated with that disease, which is a product of acute malnutrition. I had seen surgical procedures as complex as the removal of an appendix carried out with razor blades replacing scalpels and no anaesthetic whatsoever. Using these and other ready-to-hand implements our two doctors and two medical orderlies did their best to save lives which were, in truth, beyond saving. But they did all in their power. Against immense odds and against the thwarting of their efforts by the Japanese, they pursued their vocation and I saluted them.

Dempsey was struck down, for a time, by a mysterious debilitating illness, but was soon back down the mine and mixing his sweat with mine. He mixed his profanities with my own also as we seethed with rage at the abuse, physical and mental, meted out by the guards. Almost alone among us, Taffy was largely unmolested. The Japs seemed to fear mental affliction and avoided him where possible, cursing loudly in Nipponese as he stared at them with dull and morose eyes. His Changi beating continued to affect him in this way.

As our period of imprisonment lengthened, burials became more commonplace. They seemed to take place almost daily on the bleak hillside outside the camp. The guards sought to humiliate their captives even beyond the grave as they snarled '*Speedo! Speedo!*' while the plain boxes were lowered into hastily dug holes. The coffins often rested directly upon the rough planks of previous burials and were covered with the minimum of soil, accompanied to their rest without dignified prayer. The contempt and inhumanity of the guards only emphasized, we judged, that they were not as we were – a different sort of people altogether.

With our confinement in the mine, the healthy tan we had acquired on the burning plains of India and under the more temperate sun of Malaya had gone and was now replaced by a sickly pallid colour. This was emphasized by the arrival in our midst of newcomers from camps elsewhere, usually on the south side of the island. Their previous treatment by their captors had been harsh and brutal; their regime one of near starvation. They, too had suffered brutality and their wary, haggard appearance confirmed this. But they had done so in daylight, sun and fresh air. Their bronzed torsos contrasted wildly with the pallor of our own. They soon came to know the horrors of the Kinkasaki mine; the back-breaker and the heart-breaker.

Even the trek to the mine was brutally demanding as we trudged, stumbled and staggered along rocky mountain paths on painful and blistered feet before work began.

The Japanese recognized rank. NCOs were sent to work in a slightly cooler part of the mine. There were no comfortable places but some were less hellish than others.

And so the hours accumulated into days and days into weeks, which in turn gave way to months. The burials continued as exhausted and dispirited, beaten men succumbed to berri-berri, dysentery and other fatal illnesses as well as to mining accidents. Malnourishment and repeated violence was taking its toll too on minds as well as on bodies. The coarse and vibrant conversations I had enjoyed with my comrades almost ceased as we became dull and lethargic in mind and body.

We saw little of the prisoners in the other huts. Moving around the camp was held to be dangerous. If a prisoner passed a guard, he was required to bow. If the guard was unhappy with the quality of the bow, the prisoner would be reminded with a rifle butt. These beatings often took on a most savage character. On several occasions, prisoners waking in the night to use the latrines would fail, as I had, to see a guard standing in the shadows. The first announcement of the guard's presence was the impact of a rifle butt upon a frail and weakened body.

We were the living dead and social activity declined almost completely. I felt some temporary relief at the second Christmas of our stay at the mining camp when our captors unexpectedly granted permission for a concert-type get-together. It was a slight affair with a little singing and some melodeon playing. In many ways the highlight was a small banana which we received as a Christmas present. Some of the men were so hungry that they ate the skin. The get-together was a small diversion from our usual dull existence but brightened our lives a little for the couple of hours involved. We sang our songs with fervour and I felt a surge of patriotic fervour as we finished the brief interlude with Elgar's 'Land of Hope and Glory.' This was a sort of medicine – for a time – then it was back to our drudgery again and the dreary dullness of our young lives growing drearier and duller than ever.

Big Jim Powell, a Gunner in the 155th Field, missed this occasion. He was very ill and had not even received the Christmas present of the banana. He died in November 1943, as I remember. Tall and well built and never offensive to anyone, he was always well-mannered and pleasant. I would visit him in the hospital hut in the evening to spend a few minutes of my time with him as he worsened by the day. He eventually died the death of so many of our chaps, who just couldn't take the despair and hopelessness of our circumstances any more, and gave up the ghost. I felt so sorry for Jim, a pleasant-natured giant of a man compared to the diminutive thuggish bastards who reduced him to the wreck he became before the compassionate hand of Death saved him from further humiliation. I mention Jim because I remember him so well. I accuse the Japanese of the murder of Jim Powell as I accuse them of the murder of the other POW's who died at Kinkasaki. The systematic brutality, starvation and slavery in the conditions under which we all worked amounted to murder in the first degree.

Since the very first day upon which we had gone down the mine and experienced the searing heat which left our green pack-sheet shirts and shorts soaked with sweat, most of us had resorted to working naked except for a skimpy piece of material which adorned our loins. We did this in the hope that while we worked in the holes our pack-sheet togs would dry a little after our rainy journey across the mountainside each morning. We hoped for a little comfort each evening during our journey back to camp after our labours each day. This did not really work since the damp, humid conditions of the mine kept them wet; cold and wet when we donned them next morning. At least it prevented them wearing out. We had been warned by the Japanese to look after them; there would be no replacements.

95

Those of us who had any material of any kind made our 'bollock-bags', as we called them, and gave the surplus to any unfortunate who had none, so that they could be 'in the fashion', so to speak, and preserve a vestige of manly modesty. Time and the continual wear and tear of the copper ore and the ragged baskets, forever rubbing against us took their toll. The strips became threadbare and then developed gaping holes. At first we reversed them, with the tattered part at the rear, which preserved them for longer. But nothing is forever down the mine, material or life, and soon, and then for the rest of our time there, most of us worked totally naked. Well, we were treated like animals and animals go naked, so that was appropriate.

★   ★   ★

I can see myself now in that terrible dehydrating heat; the sweat pouring from every pore in our bodies. Shuffling, stark-naked POWs tottered to-and-fro carrying their baskets of hot, wet copper ore to the chutes. The ore was thrown onto the chutes and arrived at the bogey wagons below. The spluttering, flickering carbide lamps threw obscene shadows on the walls of the 'hole'. I remember, too, the times when tormented, absolutely fatigued, men lost their balance and toppled into the chute with the basket. The abrasions and mortal hurts that were received were enough to gain eternal peace on the bleak, rain-swept hillside a few hundred yards from the camp. They rested with so many others; victims of the murderous mine.

What a tragic spectacle those visions of persecution and humiliation present to me now. I grieve for my comrades at Kinkasaki who had neither the luck nor the resources of spirit to enable them to survive their degrading ordeal. The awful plight of formerly healthy young men, aloof to the threat of death on the battlefield, appals me yet. They had been reduced to Zombies, cowed and humbled by callous demons; degraded by the evil subjects of His Imperial Godless Majesty Hirohito, Emperor of Japan, and his malign mentor, Tojo san.

It was such an ignoble end which brought brave young men to a dark and gloomy hillside in the depressing mountains of Northern Formosa. No medals for these unfortunate soldiers of Great Britain; little sympathy for King George's most patriotic subjects either. They were dishonoured by historians and sullied by accusations of a lack of valour. They carried the stigma of great Britain's greatest military disgrace; but how full of valour were those who fought in the débâcle of the Malayan campaign. The failure of that campaign was not caused by any failure on the battlefield but on tea and brandy-stained maps in deep air-raid shelters. Military strategists dug trenches, underestimated the capability and armour of the Japanese and immaturely considered Singapore and Malaya to be impregnable – from the sea. The Japanese military, having done their homework properly, attacked 'through the back door,' via Thailand *and* by sea. No glory, then, for the brave men who gave their all? They were victims of history which, as all know, is controlled by historians.

Even at life's darkest moments, the human soul can throw shafts of light into the deepest gloom. Our resilience sometimes emerged in strange ways.

One such incident comes to mind. We were having our mid-shift rice break one day down the mine. Little Nobby Whitbread, a hardy Cockney from Walthamstow, grinned half-heartedly at Danny Collan and asked him for a song. Danny was one of the older men in the squad, in his early thirties and from somewhere in the midlands of England. He was propped against the wall of the narrow damp tunnel which served as our rest-room. Like most of us he was tired and drooping with fatigue. He was also completely naked, apart from the sodden and tattered pasteboard helmet on his head and the upperless, useless mine boots that were on his feet. He was a sight to behold, as he gazed at Nobby with lack-lustre eyes, blinking occasionally as the dirty, acid rainwater dripped from his shapeless headpiece. And now, some of the other grimy, sweat-streaked squaddies who were sprawled in various positions of restful repose lent support to Nobby from the 'Big Smoke.'

'Come on then, Danny Boy! Give us your effin' pleasure, you old so-and so.' This and a variety of other ungracious offerings.

Lo and behold! Danny obliged. He began to give a fair re-enactment of a song and dance routine by Laurel and Hardy with spluttering carbide lamp in one hand and empty rice-box in the other . . . and grimy sweat from his recent labours in the rocky furnace above ran in slow tired rivulets down his thin, bony body and rickety legs.

'*By the light . . . of the silvery moon . . . I love to spoon . . .*' As he sang he did a soft-shoe-shuffle in lethargic time with his toneless singing and dead-pan expression. It was an unbelievable and incongruous spectacle to behold in such squalid and depressing surroundings. As Danny finished, his tired parody there was an appreciative burst of applause from all. Even, the usually dour and indifferent 'Frying Pan' our *hancho* joined in, clapping his hands. ('Frying Pan' was so named because of the temperature of the place in which we worked).

'*Joto – joto, nana-du-ku*'; he congratulated Danny's effort. Danny's number was *nana-du-ku* and this was all we were known by now – like the beasts of the field or like lots at an auction. And now our number had come up as Frying Pan called 'Time!' and we were back to the bloody ladder again, and into our back-breaking toil and the usual chase to complete our quota of bogeys. How we loved to immerse our sweating bodies occasionally in the shallow puddle of dirty – but cooler – water which lay at the end of the dead-end tunnel underneath our workhole. We revelled in the soothing coolness as we lay, totally knackered and gasping in the relatively fresher air.

I do not know how our skeletal bodies survived this daily, frequent abuse as we changed from one temperature extreme to another and as our hearts thumped away inside our rib-cages. I do not know but I marvel. Here was a wonderful example of the resilience of flesh and blood, of the perfection of creation and of the design skill of our Maker, whoever 'He' or 'She' may be. In those exacting conditions, mere skin and bone triumphed daily over physical and mental abuse as the heart and mental faculties of most of the POWs refused to 'Give up the ghost'.

Frying Pan was never absent from his location in this Number 2 level of the mine as he went his rounds of each 'Hot Spot'. He urged flagging prisoners to greater efforts, using his punitive hammer on any unfortunate who did not measure up to his demands. No sick 'Passenger' would receive any sympathy either but would be prodded and harassed with the hammer, with the usual accompaniment of '*Speedo-speedo . . . Hakko-hakko. Yasume no' okay! Dammi-Dammi!*'. There was never any quarter given by our vile task-master as he, in turn, strove to please his Japanese masters with his output of copper ore each day.★

★ Frying Pan would later be tried as a war criminal and given a grossly inadequate sentence.

The rhythm of the days had become established. Half an hour's slavery in the terrible heat of the hole and a quick flounder down the ladder for five minutes in the muddy puddle. Then up again into the suffocating blanket of searing heat. Every day! Up and down! Up and down!

A tapping on the compressed air pipe which was situated at the top of the ladder, would signal, at last, the end of the day's work. No time was lost as we went down into the main tunnel, donned our damp, pack-sheet clothes and waited for whatever fate had in store for each of us. We wondered if our tally of bogeys was short and did not look forward to the *hancho's* summing up when he returned from the marking board where the tally for the day, from each hole, was marked up.

Never a day went past without some poor squad being found to be short of a bogey or two. There were bizarre occasions when there was not even enough ore blasted from the rock faces by the blasters for the workers to fulfil their quota; it made no difference to bloody Frying Pan! He would rant and rave and wave his hammer. The squad in question would be lined up and made to hold on to the compressed air pipes so that Bastard Frying Pan could lay into the backs of their thin, bony legs and buttocks.

One particular day in late 1944 was an especially memorable one. The squad that worked in *nee pan hachni* (Number 8 Hole) was one bogey short. Poor Danny Callan, who, such a short time ago, had raised my spirits with his rendering of '*Silvery Moon*' stood flinching at Frying Pan's hammer and trying hard to control the humiliating sobs that racked his frail body. It was a dreadful sight to see and there was nothing to be done about it by us except to stand there watching. Inside, we who watched this act of appalling brutality felt relief that on that day, at least, we had been excluded from that barbarous treatment.

On such occasions my faith failed and I wondered at the absence of my Creator. Why did He/She, Allah or Buddha, or whatever god presided, allow these monsters to humiliate His/Her mortal subjects? Dempsey and I gave a helping hand to Danny as he shuffled his way from the mine and up and down the tortuous steps outside. There was no word of consolation as we stumbled our way back to camp; we no longer had the natural energy to give solace to our comrades. At this stage all our concern was directed towards ourselves. Time was running out for us at this place of impending death and we prayed for the Yanks to rescue us from our purgatory of despair and debasement before it was too late.

Each day I looked at my worsening berri-berri and at the thinly encased ribs which grew in prominence with every weakening ordeal in the mine and with the hunger which gripped us all. I wondered if I could 'make it'. Each night, as I laid my head on my little canvas pillow, filled with rice husks, I would beseech Him to intervene on my behalf and give me salvation from the perilous ledge on which I was balanced so precariously. Each night I tugged at my forelock and hoped that my cry would be heard.

The only escape from our drudgery was the few hours of sleep we were allowed. We were only allowed sleep after nine o'clock and, if caught lying down before then, were subjected to a savage beating by the sadists who guarded us. Even then we were not always allowed to sleep in peace since, more often than not, our tormentors would storm into whatever billet they took a fancy to and hold an impromptu 'Tenko'. Woe betide any bleary-eyed POW who called out Ni instead of Si or Ku instead of Ju by mistake. The fiendish 'goons', as we called the Taiwanese guards who were the usual night-duty culprits, would excel in their vile brutality and the unfortunate miscreant would be assaulted with the usual vicious verbal and physical abuse aided by the inevitable boot and rifle butt.

At about this time Wakiyama left Kinkasaki to be replaced by Captain Immamura. We were glad at first until we discovered that Immamura was a bloody sight worse. 'No rest for the wicked'; or so the saying goes. In that case the poor abandoned soldiers of His Majesty, Geordie Boy, must, indeed have been the disciples of the Devil. We were allowed little rest by those little Taiwanese bastards. These, the lackies and dogsbodies of Tojo's troops, were on the bottom rung of the status ladder in the Nipponese ratings system. We had not even reached that rung! We were, therefore, fair game for the obnoxious swine as they passed on to us what had been given to them by the Japanese. It seemed to make them feel important to knock us about. We were taller, defenceless, degutted and inferior. All we could do was accept what they dished out and hang our cowed heads lest they might see the venom that filled our eyes.

I have heard that one can get used to anything in time. Well, I never got used to Kinkasaki, to the vile treatment I received there or to the copper mine. Neither did any of my comrades, for that matter. However if one had to be in a rough spot there was no better way to do it than in the company of the British squaddie and especially, with no thought of vanity in my mind, with the 155th Field Regiment. However black the gloom, there was always the possibility of a lighter shade of grey to lighten it with some gritty humour.

Dempsey, our 'passenger' and myself were working in a hole in the mine one day. Gunner Ponsonby, as well as his chronic asthma, had chronic diarrhoea and was too ill to be able to descend the ladder to relieve himself in the tunnel. Each time that he had to respond to the call of nature, he did what had to be done on a basket of ore and threw the offending mess into the chute and so, eventually, into the bogey at the bottom. All was well until Frying Pan happened along and decided to investigate the contents of the bogey. As he poked around in the ore, both his hammer and his hands became soiled with Ponsonby's vile offering. When Frying Pan realized what had happened, he began to scream and gesticulate like someone demented. He then began to climb the ladder, bellowing '*Gerri-gerri. Dammi, dammi. Chute shite no okay*!' We stood waiting and sweating, knowing that severe retribution was soon to follow.

'*Bagerro. Chute shite no okay. Dammio!*' His ranting went on and on until he finally stood before us and began to lay into us with his hammer, still screaming as he brutalized us. Poor Ponsonby got an extra dose when Frying Pan realized that he had been the culprit and eventually sank to the ground, sobs wracking his body, under the weight of the assault upon him.

The *hancho* finally left us alone and we did our best to contain our own sufferings and comfort Ponsonby, who was in a much worse state than we were. Frying Pan's hammer had left its punishing marks on his frail legs and emaciated, frail body. But only a part of us felt sorrow for him. We, too, had felt the weight of Frying Pan's hammer and felt compassion for ourselves also. This was how things were in Kinkasaki. We were trying to survive this hellish situation of constant hunger, hammerings and hardship. We helped one another whenever we could but when circumstances became extraordinarily severe, heroics did not happen. Survival was at the top of the agenda. A dreadful state of affairs, but the essence of grim reality.

However, many a dark cloud has a ray of golden sunshine within it and this latest encounter with Frying Pan provided much morbid, lighthearted laughter in our normally morose midst. When none of the guards were within earshot, some wag would shout out '*Chute shite. Dammi effin' dammi. Benjo no okay.*' Crude, distasteful banter in the depths of dire despair and hopelessness. But the laughter was a tonic for us – even Ponsonby was able to laugh as we visualized Frying Pan in his polluted, contaminated state.

But Ponsonby, failing fast from his ordeals, was not to smile for long and died shortly after his humbling experience in *ni pan hachi* work-hole. This *ni pan* (Number 2 level) was the hottest level in the mine and our Number 2 squad slaved in this furnace for the whole of our imprisonment at Kinkasaki. Heat in the holes ranged upwards from 130 degrees.

Every month, our cooks provided us with a little treat – burnt rice scraped from the large woks. We regarded this burnt offering as a great delicacy. We were *real* coolies now.

At about this time, Dempsey and I had been working with a hammer drill in the hole. At the end of the day's work, Dempsey threw the heavy drill down into the tunnel instead of carrying it down the ladder. Unfortunately, Frying Pan arrived on the scene to witness this and we received a hammering on the spot. Worse was to come though. We were sentenced to three days in the *eiso* (ice box) back at camp.

This 5×5×5 bamboo cage was situated in front of the Japs' guard-room. Unless you were very small, it was impossible to stand upright. However, you were not allowed to sit or lie down to ease the strain. If the Japs caught you doing either, you would be doused with cold water and prodded and whacked with bamboo poles until you were upright again. After the three days were over, between the complete lack of sleep and the terrible strain on our legs and bodies, we were in a state of complete exhaustion of mind and body. This experience had taken a terrible toll of us and, thinner and more gaunt than ever, we were back down the mine the next day, with Dempsey swearing vengeance. I fervently hoped that he would get his wish because the only way that we would get vengeance was if the Americans or British invaded Formosa and set us free.

As though in answer to our constant prayer, a glimmer of hope appeared in the skies in the shape of huge American bombers by both day and night. There was, at last, a lifting of the despair which was so deeply ingrained within me, as the vision of freedom from our oppressive confinement appeared in the heavens above. I kept my fingers crossed that our friends, the Yanks, would not bomb us. The camp was not marked in any way. They didn't.

We were now put to work blasting a new tunnel. There was much surprise and great relief, when we paraded for work one morning, to find that we were to be spared the toil of the trek up and down the rugged hillside. Instead we were marched to the rear of the camp and through an opening in the rock face. We realized, with surprise, that we were in the tunnel that we had been working for some weeks now. I had wondered what was behind the blasting of the tunnel and was very pleased at the outcome. This would remove the misery of those steps and the burden of carrying our sick comrades to and from the hellish pit. We would also be saved from the wettings on the way from the prevailing cold drizzle which kept our pack-sheet clothes forever sodden and so uncomfortable to wear. The other bonus was to get into the mine quicker and out of the way of annihilation at the hands of our own airmen during the, by now, constant raids on the island. It is strange to record our view of the mine as a protector, strange that a place against which the tortured slaves of ancient Rome would have rebelled, should be seen to offer sanctuary.

Our conditions had not improved but we could bear the hammerings and intimidation with greater fortitude since we believed that it might not be for long now. The Yanks would arrive, cavalry style, and free us all soon . . . well free those of us who were left.

We were in a really bad way by now. Our berri-berri worsened and acute diarrhoea took its toll of the sparse flesh that remained stretched thinly across our protruding bones. Dysentry raged too and we had been close to despair; abandonment of all hope; the total loss of will to live and the final dreadful solution of embracing the compassionate grasp of death itself. Now, with the arrival of the bombers, each day became a day to be survived and night became a time in which to wonder about what the next day might bring at the hands of our tormentors. I prayed earnestly, as I laid my head on my hard pillow, that I might be allowed to live to greet our saviours, the GI's. I implored my Lord and my Lady to look on me with compassion and give me the extra strength to keep me going.

The reader may wonder, or feel surprise, that soldiers trained for war would accept the treatment meted out to us by the Japanese without response. He or she may wonder that we could watch the humiliation and barbarity meted out by our captors to our mates without interfering. The reader should wonder no more. We knew the vile moods of our captors. We had seen their willingness to use hobnailed boots, rifle butts and anything to hand in pursuit of their ends. We also knew their willingness to use bullets and bayonets, if the occasion merited, and to use them without remorse. But most of all we knew that a show of resistance in the circumstances would achieve only the certain death of anyone who intervened, as well as the certain death of those on whose behalf we did so.

Even escape from this island hell of blood and sweat was not possible. In a population of orientals, a Westerner was visible and that visibility would lead, inescapably, to certain death. We were young men who had given our youth for King and country. We wanted desperately to survive these demanding, demeaning, miserable days.

We became reduced to the servile category of Zombies or mindless automatons. We were stripped of our clothing but of much more besides. Our commandant had promised that we would be treated like coolies, and so we were. We were empty shells like oysters from which the pearl had been removed. Fight and resistance were excised. Perhaps we can be forgiven for our lack of resistance during the criminal abuse of our colleagues . . . and of ourselves!

*　　*　　*

After more than three years of captivity, we were on our last legs. Every minute was precious to us as we strove to keep alive for our hoped for liberation. From the young, naïve man who had volunteered for the Lanarkshire Yeomanry in 1939, I was now a well matured man with a wealth of experience behind me. (Some of that experience I would willingly have sacrificed.) And, I was still alive when so many of my comrades had died horrific deaths. So why should I complain? There was light for me now in this abyss of despair.

When I thought of the new tunnel into the mine and the saving of effort which it would bring about, I wondered whether the Japs were beginning to show some consideration for us in our weakened state.

But I should have known better, I should have known that there would be an ulterior motive behind the making of that cavern.

During our goings and comings each day, I had noticed holes drilled along the full length of the sides and the roof of the tunnel and had assumed that these holes were to permit the enlarging of the tunnel at some point. Then, Taiwanese workers installed thick, reinforced doors at each end of the tunnel and everyone wondered at the purpose of these. Why had the Japs put these very strong, iron banded doors at the entrance and exit to the tunnel? We were not left to wonder for long. A civilian Taiwanese worker in the mine informed us that the tunnel was to be our tomb if the Americans, who were bombing Taiwan day and night, invaded the island. At the first sign of invasion, the POWs were to be herded into the tunnel and the heavy doors at each end closed and bolted. And the holes which had been drilled would be primed with explosives and detonated – burying us under thousands of tons of copper ore – and leaving no trace of us or the atrocities which had been committed on us.

We had worked in this mine for two and a half years, not knowing when – or if – we would be free. During that time, the thought of eventual freedom was all that we had to cling to. Our hearts would rejoice when we saw the American planes overhead and listened to them bombing our enemy, hoping – and expecting – that these bombing raids meant that the end of our torment might not be too far away. And now, to hear that we would never be free – that death *was* to be our only escape from the mine and, the final bitter irony, that we would actually be buried in it. That, in trying to rescue us, the Americans would actually be signing our death warrant!

Once again, I beseeched God to listen to my pleas for redemption from this plight and, Alleluiah!, my prayers were answered.

★   ★   ★

One day, as we paraded for work, the *Buncho Dono* appeared with the little, fat interpreter and told us that we would not be going down the mine again. We would be going to another camp on the island. His normally expressionless face was clouded with displeasure as he turned on his heel and disappeared as quickly as he had come. Had one of his superiors forbidden his plan to 'leave no trace' of us? We would never know.

105

This bolt from the blue took some time to sink in but eventually, as we were dismissed and sent back to our huts, the reality dawned – no more descending into the pit of Kinkasaki's hell. No more Level Number 2! No more the humiliation of watching the beatings! No more flinching under the blows from the long hammer as it bruised legs swollen with berri-berri or bare, bony backsides! No more struggles to control convulsive weeping! No more terror as we awaited the arrival of the *hancho* when we had not fulfilled our quotas! No more slithering down the wet and grimy ladders to immerse our sweating bodies in the water that gathered at the side of the bogey rail while our hearts pounded and steam rose from us!

All that misery was behind us now – as long as this was not yet another of the Japs' tricks. I prayed that it was not and honoured the compassion of God by silent gratitude for our deliverance from evil.

That same day we were on parade once more, with the guards picking out the sickest of us. They were issued with their boots and, carrying their meagre personal possessions, were marched from the camp to take up residence in camps on other parts of the island. As one of the two or three hundred who were left behind, I never got to know where they were taken. I never saw them again.

Then we, who were becoming apprehensive as to what our fate was to be, were issued also with the boots that we had been relieved of so long ago and began to clear the camp of all rice and other assorted stores. We carried this to the minehead and loaded it into small mining wagons. This task, even, took its toll on us. We had to trudge up and down all those tortuous steps on the steep mountainside. What a bloody state our feet were in with painful blisters from the stiff unyielding leather which had not been used for so many months.

We staggered and stumbled back and forth with the stores and cursed the bellowing and constant abuse from the Japanese guards and from the goons. Our bleeding toes and ankles cried out for medication which was denied them.

Then came the welcome day when all was accounted for and we were allowed a much needed respite. We were able to bathe our feet with soothing cold water since no other medication was, of course, available. We nevertheless fully appreciated the gift of clean water we had received from Mother Nature.

During this period we were not allowed to leave our huts except

106

to visit the latrine. This restriction was caused by the constant daily bombing of the island by the United States Air Force. We could see clearly the alarm on the faces of the guards, who continued to respond with the thuggishness we had seen throughout. Our reaction was much changed. The lips which had drooped in sheer hopelessness, now became very stiff in typical British style. We endured stoically and we listened to the passing of heavily laden B29 bombers. Their deadly cargoes having been dropped on near and far corners of Formosa, we heard their return and passing. We continued to worry about the lack of markings to identify the camp as a POW compound and hoped fervently that they would not destroy us as well.

★   ★   ★

Our 'Yasume' passed all too quickly and our keepers had us on the move again with whatever personal belongings we had. We found ourselves on the way back along the rugged and tortuous trek on which we had suffered so much so long ago. As before, we were pushed and punched and kicked mercilessly onwards. When one of us fell, the boot and the butt were dispensed liberally.

Nothing is forever and five or so hours later, with the rocky road, Kinkasaki and the copper mine well behind us, we reached the little village at the end of the railway track. We piled gratefully on to the ancient train which awaited us there out of the way, for now at least, of the screaming abusive guards. The hard wooden seats offered a welcome rest to our weary, aching bodies.

I thought of those I had left behind; brave men who had given their lives and who sought, and were given, nothing in return. I remembered the rough planking I had seen so many times which encased their emaciated, desecrated flesh. They lay in unconsecrated ground, and few words have been spoken to honour them. There was no glory for these poor souls; the abandoned flotsam of war.

I prayed again and thanked my Creator for deliverance thus far. As before, I included Buddha, Krishna and Mohammed but as to that Shinto chappie, he was a bloody Japanese bastard like the rest of his brethren on earth.

I had never been fortunate enough to be selected on one of the 'Thin man' parades and thus fulfil my earnest wish to be free of the mine. I was one of eighty-odd prisoners who had spent the entire punishing three years there and I was still alive, albeit weighing only six stones. I was still alive though, so really I couldn't complain . . . Well?

Everything would be better now. We would enjoy the sun and the fresh air which would put healthy colour into our dirty, yellow-stained bodies. Perhaps I might even put on a pound or two in the new camp. The future might be rosy. Time would tell. We were crossing the fence and would soon find out the colour of the grass on the other side. Fate would deal the cards. Surely we would be dealt a royal flush instead of the deuces of the past.

I savoured every mile of that journey as the train took me further from the dark heathen mountainside on which lay buried my friends and comrades whose sweat had mixed with my own in the hellish pit at Kinkasaki.

6

The Jungle Camp of Kukutsu

The screeching of brakes on the train wheels woke me, after a session of spiritual kow-towing with my Maker. I was brought to ground level and grim reality with a juddering impact. We had reached the end of the line. Through the carriage window I spied a large notice with Chinese characters on it and underneath these the word, in more familiar lettering, Taihoku. We could now see clear signs that the American bombers had been busy. I enjoyed a quiet sense of revenge.

The guards came running along the length of the train, banging on the doors with their rifle butts. (A welcome change from banging them on us). They screamed for us to dismount – which we did smartly, having no wish to be last out and suffer the penalty for it – the inevitable battering from the guards' boots and fists and the brass butts of their Lee Enfields.

Such a bizarre situation, we thought, which could only happen to us. To worry about unjust chastisement from the 'best of British' brass. The lethal weapons were the produce of our own country and of the Birmingham Small Arms Company. Irony indeed! But I suppose that's life; a lucky dip. We felt, at the time though that the dips were more often unlucky. I suppose too that we just have to accept with a philosophical mind that the unseen hand, which orders these things, does so in an unbiased way.

We were counted again and again in accordance with the usual blustering ritual and then hurriedly hustled through the side streets of the town to where another dilapidated train awaited us. We were bundled unceremoniously on board by the impatient guards and were soon on our way once more, leaving behind us the piles of rubble and bombed buildings and, I suppose, a fair number of Taihoku's dead.

We actually got out only just in time. We could see troops and civilians running in panic-stricken disorder to seek safety from a large formation of B29 US bombers which could be heard and seen overhead. If we had been a few minutes later, well . . .. At last we seemed to have received one of Fate's favours.

The Thud! Thud! of exploding bombs filled the air as the bombers continued to raze the city. So powerful were the explosions that we could feel the carriages juddering with each impact. We thought of the brutality of the forced march through the rugged mountain country and away from the camp. We remembered the studied indifference of the pitiless guards to our injuries. We considered their unconcern for the suffering and agony of blistered feet. And we pondered their contempt for the aches in our backs because of the extra loads we carried. They had taken pleasure in denying us even the briefest rest. How strange, then, that their very cruelty should have been instrumental in our deliverance from this mass bombing in Taihoku. The few minutes saved now seemed to us to be very precious and important.

I rejoiced at the continued sounds of explosions as we left them behind. I thought again of 'tugging my forelock' but refrained from doing so lest I should be deemed to have overdone my grovelling but I did give silent thanks for the B29 bomber. The Yanks weren't coming. They were here. Soon we would be free.

Half an hour later, the old locomotive shuddered to a halt at a terminus. We found ourselves at a small village called Shinten, situated at the foot of some thickly wooded, mountainous terrain. The guards were back to their repetitive screaming and we were hurriedly ejected from the carriages. The last out got the usual treatment. We were counted again and again and then marched to a nearby warehouse where each of us were given supplies to carry to wherever our new 'campo' was to be. My load was a sackful of rice. (half a hundredweight). The population of Shinten, dressed in their drab, cotton clothes watched apathetically as the guards hustled us onto a narrow path which led upwards into the hills.

110

As the last chapter clearly showed, the mine had taken a grim toll of us. Each step upward on the tortuous, torturing and rugged path was agony. Our bleeding feet added to that agony. To add to our torment, the dense, overhanging jungle foliage seemed to retain an airless humidity, which taxed our lungs and hearts and seemed to suck the sweat from our pores. The sweat streamed in rivulets swamping and stinging our eyes and blinding us as we staggered on. As had become normal for us, woe betide anyone who dropped his load, even from sheer physical or mental exhaustion. The brutish, scowling guards would at once lay in with kicks and rifle butts.

After an hour and a half of cruel, constant uphill struggle the Corporal in charge, a stranger to us with a mean, sullen face adorned by a Hitler-type moustache, bellowed '*Yasume! – skoshi Yasume!*' The relief was instantaneous and a blessing to us all. We promptly dropped our loads and ourselves to the rock-strewn ground.

Every bone in me was protesting at the want of rest and I longed to remove my boots from my lacerated feet. They felt as though a fierce fire burnt within them, which called for dousing with clear cool water. I slouched beside the rice only too well aware that if I once took them off I would not be able to put them back on again. Common sense prevailed and I had to continue to suffer them; there was nothing else to do.

Time seemed to be the eternal enemy! After about ten minutes of blissful relaxation on the hard earth, the sadistic looking corporal strode up and down the line screaming. (We later christened him Tashi). He brandished a stout length of bamboo. '*Yasume sunda!* (Rest Finished) *Speedo! Speedo! Hakko! Hakko!*'

Those who did not respond to his satisfaction found themselves at the wrong end of that intimidating rod. The rest of the guards seemed wary of him and anxious to please their new master. The easy way to do this seemed to be to become even more brutal than ever.

We were again beasts of burden and liable to be treated as such and unable to act, on our own behalf, against this. We were cowed and in the yoke, which we bore in silence.

Robert Burns had written 'A man's a man for a' that'. Robert had clearly never encountered life, as my comrades and I had, at the hands of the Japanese military. If he had his immortal lines would never have been written. These beings who shared our planet and who could

111

thrust a sponge, impregnated with sulphuric acid, into an open wound were not men, as we had known them. They were bloody demons and fiends; more vicious than the jackal or hyena that haunts the jungle; monsters, neither more nor less.

After another hour, we reached a large clearing in the jungle which was to be our new home. We piled the stores into a roughly made hut. Next to it, beside the entrance to another smaller hut was our camp commander from Kinkasaki watching us and smiling a contemptuous smile. We stumbled past him.

Immamura was no better than the guards he presided over and was never slow to show his disgust at our appearance. There was to be no compassion shown to us. He had made it plain that he regarded us as cowards by giving up the battle for Malaya and Singapore. Nippon would never surrender to anyone he had assured us when he had first addressed us back at Kinkasaki. The brave soldiers of Japan would never become coolies such as he would make us. We now knew that even though we would be free of the mine, with its hot holes and humiliations, our backs would surely be bent as before. He would find some demeaning work for us to pass the time away and be better able to do so with the aid of his evil tempered Japanese corporal, Tashi.

The camp had no fence; none was required. We were too high up in the almost impenetrable jungle to even think of escape in our weakened state. Tashi announced that we could have 'skoshi yasume' but added that if anyone attempted to escape he would immediately be shot. That made little difference since we knew that anyway. Moreover, with the Yanks so near and the great prospect of rescue before very long, we were even more unlikely to take the risk.

A stream of fresh water cascaded from the heights of the mountain and a fairly large pool lay invitingly at the edge of the clearing. We lost no time in easing the boots from our wounded feet and crowding into the, much dreamt of, cool, clear water. We splashed about in this balm, the gift of Mother Nature, and revelled in the caressing ripples of this embrocation from the surrounding uplands. The mountains back at Kinkasaki had been bleak and barren and in keeping with the harshness of the mine's interior. Here the lush abundance of trees, shrubbery and tall elephant grass produced a palette of wonderful shades of green and was soothing to our eyes. The jungle camp already seemed to be paradise in comparison to the melancholy drabness of

Kinkasaki. We had the open sky above us and the sun as our constant companion; rather than the dark, insecure roofs and searing heat.

I was prepared to like it here, I was thinking. The sun would soon disperse the dirty yellowish stains with which the mine's acid water had covered us and replace it with a healthy tan. The fresh air would breathe new life into tired lungs.

How wonderful it was to treat our swollen painful feet to the alleviating natural anaesthetic of the cold water. We made the most of it until Tashi arrived with one of his scowling henchmen and we had to leave our paradise and line up to be counted again. We did this in the brisk manner demanded by our masters: – *ichi; nee; san; si; goh; rokko; sichi; hachi; ku; ju;* – and so on until the last prisoner shouted the final number. The occasional blunder was rewarded by a crack on the head from Tashi's bamboo rod and angry reprovals, which were delivered in the usual way. '*Dammi-Dammi, bagerro, no okay!*'

The fat interpreter showed up then, still sweating profusely from his struggle up the rough mountain path and told us we would cut down trees from the surrounding jungle and build our own huts. The abundant elephant grass would be used to thatch the roof. Until then we would sleep on the ground, with the starry sky for a ceiling. So our first task would make us lumberjacks and this didn't sound too bad to me. A doddle, I thought, by comparison to the mine.

We were issued with two blankets apiece, which we had brought with us, and being bone tired we lost little time in spreading ourselves upon the sun-baked earth. I was filled almost with ecstasy as I lay down with those two rough army blankets to keep the chill of night at bay. For me the earth was as good as a feather mattress and the bed fit for any King. I again thanked God as I drifted into sleep. No dreams I dreamt!

I was wakened abruptly by the sound of screaming as Tashi's men made their presence only too evident. I assembled with the others and we went on parade. I was placed in a grass cutting squad along with Taffy and Dempsey. We were given rusty sickles and machetes. Only when the guards were satisfied were we allowed to attend to our basic ablutions and to visit the open trench which had been dug at the clearing edge and which was to serve as a latrine.

A ration of a handful of boiled rice was given to us along with some lukewarm water to swill the tasteless but welcome food down. All the while the churlish guards were snarling at us in their usual brutal way. They hurried us to our place of work. We, the grass-cutting party, went to the place where the tall elephant grass grew most abundantly, about half a mile from the camp, while the tree-cutters, armed with axes and rusting log-saws, went searching for suitable timber to construct the huts. Throughout this time the balmy morning air was adulterated with the guttural and abusive commands of the guards as they hurried their charges onwards to begin their day's toil.

We reached the tall grass and Tashi, with whose presence we were unlucky to be burdened, made it clear from the start that 'Yasume' was not a word we would often hear. We were all too well acquainted with the weight of Frying Pan's hammer should we be found slacking – or even accused of slacking. Tashi had made it clear that, as far as he was concerned, we were out of the Frying Pan and into the fire. We set to work hacking at the tough, tall grass, which had stems as thick as your finger. We had to chop it with the rusty, blunt tools we had been given. Any scrawny but unbent back was dealt with immediately by the scowling and vicious Japanese NCO with his bamboo stick. Notions of easier days were soon dispelled and in double quick time.

Our youth had been stolen and with it had gone much of our resilience. We were expected to provide, on demand, the energy that Tashi and his bloodstained bamboo called for and could not do so. The blood on his rod was that of the unfortunates who fell by the wayside.

The punishing labour went on as we tried to avoid Tashi's beatings by stretching our wills to breaking point, a task made the more difficult by his resentment at the regular appearance in the skies of the twin-fuselage aircraft bearing the white star of the USA. He sank to lower depths of depravity, as the US warplanes bombed at will with never a Japanese Zero in the air to challenge them. But as they had an effect upon him so too did they affect us. They provided the stimulus to keep going and their daily visits were a tonic to us, setting morale upon an upward spiral again. In contrast, Tashi would fall into a cowardly rage that made him even more bestial than before.

Occasionally, some of us allowed our approval of the actions of our US friends to show and even this mild show of resistance was dealt with severely. The offenders were made to kneel on the ground while a piece of wood was placed at the back of their knees. They were made to sit back causing intense pressure in this area and an effective blockage in the blood supply. After a short time the legs were left bereft of feeling. Tashi then commanded them to stand and maintain an impossible upright stance, impossible because of the numbness of the already weakened limbs. When they fell he would batter them with his rod across legs and buttocks, shoulders and head. And he would laugh his evil laugh as his poor, painwracked victim cowered before him, trembling, attempting to maintain an erect position on incapacitated legs but usually unable to do so. His underlings would attempt to ingratiate themselves with him by laughing and jeering.

Watching one of these sessions, Dempsey was unable to contain himself. 'Bloody Japanese bastards' he swore quietly as a young Englishman was trying to stifle uncontrollable sobbing against a background of the barbarian contempt of the Japanese. Tashi heard the forbidden words and went raving mad, ranting and swearing in abusive Nipponese and glaring at Dempsey. While the Japs converged upon Dempsey, the young Englishman was left alone and began to compose himself. Dempsey, on the other hand, knew he had blundered and knew what was to follow but, though as weakened as the rest of us, he retained a spark of wild and irrational defiance, which did not allow him to do other than stand his ground. Tashi whacked him on the head.

The mad-eyed Japanese screamed insanely, '*Bastardo – no okay. Dammi – dammi. Bastardo dammio – Bagerro, dammi – dammi*' and with each cry he bounced his rod off Dempsey. Dempsey still refused to give ground and Tashi became ever more incensed and enraged as Dempsey refused to fall and as he saw the contempt in Dempsey's eyes. Like the rest of the squad, I could do nothing but watch as the mad NCO waded in with stick and fists. I willed Dempsey to swallow his pride and go down. At last one of the henchmen succeeded where Tashi had failed. He kicked furiously at the back of Dempsey's legs, making him fall to the ground in a crumpled heap but still allowing him to contain the agony of his beating. He refused to show the usual tears of humiliation and this defiance was unbearable to Tashi, who was unable to comprehend the fact that one of the cowed and beaten men, calloused by years of starvation and humiliation, would refuse to beg for mercy under this demeaning abuse.

115

Tashi changed tack. He watched two of his lackeys kick Dempsey repeatedly. He then announced that another POW had to take part in the humiliation. This was a common depravity among them. They would make two prisoners face each other and swing punches until one of them fell. I wondered who would be chosen and fervently hoped it would not be me. I could not have punched my friend in these circumstances. Tashi, however, strode to where Taffy Morgan was and jabbed him with the bamboo rod. '*Yosh – anatowa*' he snarled at Taffy pointing to Dempsey and indicating the odious task in hand.

Taffy had still not recovered fully from his beating at Changi and was in a semi-stupor. His face was expressionless as he followed Tashi to the spot where his friend Dempsey stood, swaying weakly on quivering legs. Taffy took a long lingering look at the vicious Jap Corporal, who urged him on, bellowing the usual gutturals. Tashi jabbed a finger at Dempsey and, at last, Taffy squared up to his mate.

Dempsey raised his head, blood washing down his face, and nodded to Taffy to 'Get on with it!' He well understood the grim situation. Taffy met his friend's eye and wasted no further time. He raised his calloused right hand and thumped Dempsey with all the strength he could muster in his own weakened state. Dempsey dropped like a stone.

It was obvious to all who watched that Dempsey would not rise for a while after being hit so hard and Tashi and his gloating serfs were convulsed with laughter and clapped their hands crying '*Joto – Joto*' (Good, Good).

Taffy looked at me. As our eyes met I saw a glimmer there that had been absent for too long. His look clearly said that he had done what had to be done under the circumstances. Dempsey was having enforced rest, Tashi had been deprived of further depraved entertainment and Dempsey had surrendered to a British hand rather than a Japanese.

The NCO's thirst for cruelty having, for the moment, been slaked, he returned to normal. This of course involved screaming at POWs who had paused in their work to watch the grim spectacle. He brandished his rod as a reminder to each man that he might be next in line. Dempsey, meanwhile, was left to lie and recover consciousness without any kind of medical attention. This was how it was with the Empire of Nippon. A Japanese code of honour might have been exceedingly short.

We could have done nothing for poor Dempsey. We were intimidated and cowed. Our intervention would only have resulted in another victim on the ground beside him, just as in the copper mine we had perforce looked at our comrades suffering from Frying Pan's long shafted hammer. We had been shorn not only of energy and flesh but of our independence of mind also. We accepted persecution without whine or whimper having become but passive unresisting drudges.

'Rule Britannia'? 'Britons never, never, never shall be slaves!'?

Well look at us now!

In a surge of patriotic fervour we had volunteered to serve King and country. We had accepted one measly shilling for the services which would be rendered. Well! His noble, bloody, Majesty George had got more than his bob's worth from the poor fall-guys he had abandoned on the battlefield of Malaya. And no place of honour in the history books, which would be written, awaited them either. Friend and foe alike would brand them as cowards. Poison pens would bring them disgrace. Perhaps it would be best if they were simply forgotten!

So much for hope and glory! I had been abandoned here to rot. I remembered the advice of an old soldier – 'Never volunteer for anything'. Well it was years too late since I had already done so by joining the Lanarkshire Yeomanry and here I was, paying the bloody penalty.

Our work-filled days drove on. Paddy Flannigan, a stalwart from County Offaly in Ireland heard a rustling in the elephant grass. He immediately disappeared into it. Seconds later he emerged carrying a snake which he had beheaded with his machete. He showed it to me with a furtive grin on his leathery face then quickly hid it in the grass again. He feared that the guards might see it and take it for themselves. The shortage of food was such that they too were beginning to feel the ravages of hunger. Anything that could be eaten was a desirable target. Paddy handed the six-foot-long snake to our cooks when he returned to camp, having transported it there inside the folds of his tattered shirt.

Next day we received the snake from the cooks. It had been skinned and boiled along with the rice and cut into small pieces. Eight of the ten eggs that had been inside it were returned also. They had retained two of the eggs as a fee for their services. This welcome addition to our diet was shared among the hungry, skinny fellows in our hut (which had only that day been completed). We ate the grisly flesh of the snake and I enjoyed the solid yolk of an egg, which Paddy gave to me. I gave thanks to God for this gift. The gift was a means to an end, a purchase of time towards the eventual goal of survival. Life is sweet 'tis said! Well at around this period I felt a great bitterness. I would have needed considerable assistance from Messrs Tate and Lyle – but then so would all of us, in that jungle camp of Kukutsu.

The long days turned into weeks. The depressing agony continued as Tashi sank to depths we had not dreamed possible. He gloated over his victims and took a sadistic gratification at the sight of men cringing from his rod. Our weakness was such that the relentless burning of the sun had begun to remind us of the awful hot-holes in the mine. It seemed to be trying to put an end to our suffering and our lives.

Strangely, the day we had all been praying for came silently. There was no drama, in the camp, at the beginning of that day, 15 August, 1945. Halfway through our day's toil we stopped for our rice break. The rice was the usual handful with a few strips of pickled seaweed to garnish it. As usual, we were grateful for each tasteless grain. But, most unusually, we became aware of a change in the demeanour of the hateful guards. Normally they would have been strutting among us as we rested, grinning evilly at the state we were in and gesturing mockingly at the physique of some chosen victim. But on that day, and I say again 15 August, 1945, they kept well apart from us, gathered in a huddle but glancing frequently towards us with expressions even more hostile and sullen than usual. It was clear to us that they were uneasy about something although about what we could not fathom. We wondered most of all at the absence of the application of rod, rifle butt and boot.

As I lay on my back, exhausted, in the sun, I realized that for the first time in recent weeks the skies above our heads had been empty; not a single aeroplane had flown over that morning nor had there been any sound of aircraft in the distance. I wondered at their absence. I wondered if both phenomena were related. A strange hope began to flutter within our hearts and speculation about this or that, perhaps even of the war ending, mounted. The glimmer of light at the end of the tunnel of our despair suddenly flared and with it wild hopes and expectations of freedom at last.

'Oh to be in England, (or even better Scotland) now that Spring is here.' Fond thoughts of Caledonia occupied my mind. But the day's surprises were not yet over. We were lined up and told that '*roiki*' was over for the day. We marched back to camp in the heat of the sun and, assembled once again, we learned that the war in the East was really over.

We were dismissed by the glowering guards and made a beeline to our huts where we could enjoy relative privacy from the hated Tashi. I think to all of our surprise there was no wild jubilation at this news we had awaited so long. Our hearts were filled with gratitude that we would be free of this hellish island and its bloody copper mine. But our joy was quiet, inner joy. We sank to the ground to rest our aching bodies. One or two men were tearful and trying to hide their tears behind calloused, blistered hands. But they had no need for embarrassment or concern. None of their co-prisoners regarded their tears as 'unmanly'. We knew how they felt. Each of us was a survivor and had proved our mettle by achieving this. We had beaten the odds, which were stacked against us and could be proud of doing so. But even in this, our moment of triumph, I remembered the dead we had left behind. Neither was their death shameful. Each one of them will ever be a hero in my mind. Part of me would remain with them on the bleak, black mountain.

Dempsey lay on one side of me, completely knackered, not having fully recovered from his beating of a short time ago. Taffy was sitting on the other side with the semblance of a smile on his, normally sober, Welsh face. I could hear him saying quiet words of memory about Maggie, the girl he had left behind at Lanark. 'Maggie, Maggie.' His face lit up at the thought as he continued softly . . . 'and little Taffy . . . little Taffy Mcbloody Tavish . . . and Maggie, my Maggie'.

I had many times petitioned my Lord and my Lady hoping that they would hear my cries for deliverance. Now I knew that it had been noted and dealt with efficiently by my heavenly benefactors. This was a suitable time to offer my gratitude for services rendered.

They had shown themselves to be good friends and with no irreverence I said 'Thanks Pal!' and sincerely meant it. I could not have escaped from that bloody mess without their helping hand. I fell on my knees in special acknowledgement.

Two days later, we were told that we would be on our way in the morning to another camp on the island. This was good news as it would be one more step towards home and one more step towards freedom from the Japanese guards who were still in command of things. The day wore on. We were more or less confined to our huts, passing the time as best we could. By resting we hoped to restore some strength into our still aching and scarred bodies.

A grey shroud of evening was falling on the clearing outside the huts and as I gazed out of the gap that served as a doorway I spied a shadowy, furtive figure hurrying past and going towards the dense jungle at the rear of where our hut stood. I recognized the figure as Tashi the effin terrible, our sadistic NCO. He appeared to be carrying a loaded valise on his back and his rod in his hand. I had the feeling that he was 'fleeing the coop'. Now, as I speculated on Tashi's speedy departure, I saw another form on the move, Taffy. I thought he had been having forty winks. He had apparently seen Tashi also and he disappeared through a window opening in the side of the hut. Soon he was gone in the covering darkness, following the route that Tashi had taken. I had no time to stop him. It had all happened so suddenly and had taken me quite by surprise. I could only gasp with astonishment as the full realization of what Taffy was about sank in. Dempsey had seen it all too and began to berate the foolish action of the once burly Welshman.

'Daft Welsh bugger', Dempsey summed up as he voiced his astonishment at the action of the Welshman and I could not do other than agree with him. We knew that if he did catch Tashi he would be at a considerable physical disadvantage, because of his past ordeal at the hands of Tashi's comrades and of Tashi himself.

Both Dempsey and I stationed ourselves at the window, staring out into the darkness and hoping that our mate would turn back before any of the other guards caught sight of him. Even now they would probably shoot first and ask questions later. Luck was not with Taffy, as two Japanese sentries stopped right outside our hut and began to converse in guttural Nipponese.

There was nothing either of us could do about the complicated situation which had developed so we had to cross our fingers and hope for the best. The seconds ticked by and became minutes and the guards showed no sign of moving on. They chattered away to each other with the ends of their cigarettes glowing ominously in the dark. At that moment I could have been doing with a 'coffin nail' myself, to steady my fraying nerves as I listened intently for any sound of our foolhardy mucker returning from 'Mission Impossible'.

All was nerve-rackingly quiet then, suddenly, from out of the darkness of the surrounding jungle, there reverberated a chilling sound. If the Japanese guards did not recognize it we did. It was the sound of Morgan impersonating Johnny Weissmuller, an undulating trumpeting sound. The sound of Tarzan as he called his elephant and chimpanzee friends. Dempsey was as incredulous as anyone might expect and, indeed, as I was myself. 'Bloody Hell', he said, 'The bugger must be aff his heid. The bliddy Japs are bound to hear him.'

There was nothing to do but agree. Taffy's abuse at Changi by the cruel Japs had clearly left him a penny short of a bob . . . and here he was proving it. Again the silence of the night was broken by Taffy's wild cry. An eeriness followed with even the night-time insects of the jungle going quiet at our mate's mad call of the wild. One of the Japs identified the fearsome yodel for his comrade with apprehension in his, slightly tremulous voice. '*Tarzan san . . . No okay – dammi-dammi, Okari, joto nai.*' His companion answered '*Hai, Toriko . . . Tarzan san, hai*' revealing a good measure of fright as well. '*Dammi-dammi. Bagerro. Matti-matti, no okay! Dammio!*'

And with this they deserted their posts, ill at ease with the thought, that Tarzan san might swing through the trees and tear them asunder.

Dempsey laughed and I did too. We knew that Taffy had a chance now of returning safely – for all his bloody stupid Welsh arrogance.

Soon we heard a splash and, moments later; a figure appeared from the darkness and came through the open window. It stood before us holding out a length of stout bamboo to us. It was Taffy and he grinned jubilantly at us.

'Dead! Dead! . . . The bastard's dead', he blurted out, gasping for breath from his escapade. 'I caught him hiding in the elephant grass and grabbed the bloody stick. I battered the shit out of him with it. Squealing like a pig, he was. Begging for bloody mercy. Done the

121

bastard in, I did. Did it for you, Dempsey, for what he did to you. Bastard, bastard, bastard!' he was still in a state of excitement, 'Won't batter you any more with his bloody stick, I've got it.' Taffy brandished Tashi's stick and fresh blood could be seen streaking the length of it.

Dempsey was still concerned. 'I hope you've not left him where the bliddy Japs'll bliddy well find 'im?'

Taffy grinned triumphantly. 'I drowned the evil bastard, I did. He's at the bottom of the latrine with a big stone stuffed in his trousers to keep him down.' There was little chance of Tashi being found.

Our Welsh mate smiled with pleasure at the thought of where Tashi now '*Yasume'd*'.

'Good enough for the bloody bastard! He'll be at home there amongst our souvenirs'.

I remembered the splash and knew that Taffy had exacted an appropriate revenge for one and all of us, for what we had endured at Tashi's evil hands.

Most of the lads in the hut were up and about now and fully aware of Taffy's bold venture. They crowded all around him clapping his back in excited gratitude as they shared in the satisfaction of the moment – the satisfaction of Tashi lying in perpetual repose among such suitable farewell 'gifts' from all of them. 'Tis often said, 'Revenge is sweet'. Yet there are times when the craving of the soul for justice is denied and we must then resort to visions of retribution in the mind, accomplishing with the pen that which we have been unable to exact with the sword.

I advised Taffy to hide the bamboo rod lest it be recognized by any of them causing the finger of accusation to be pointed at him. He stroked it with affection and smiled a smile of grim satisfaction. 'Some of *his* blood on it now, Johnny boy, just as it should be. An eye for a bloody eye.' He slid the rod under his blankets and followed suit. It had been a tiring day; we all needed sleep, perhaps to dream of the evil Tashi gurgling in the depths of the foul-smelling latrine ditch.

The morning came and it was so different from past mornings. The Japanese kept their distance and left us in peace to attend to our ablutions at leisure. This basic privilege was a wonderful experience after the past years. We took our time and relished the relative freedom from tyranny. The Japs, however, were still in charge and it was not yet the time for singing. We knew the time would come and were content to wait.

As we bathed in the clear water of the little pool, the rest of the men got to know of Taffy's trophy. It added spice to the morning. As they perched on the edge of the latrine and did what they had to do they thought of Tashi being on the receiving end for once. We performed the doubly unchristian act, not of turning the other cheek but of turning the other two bloody cheeks to him! Revenge is sweet 'tis said, but no revenge was ever as sweet as ours was. A sweetener in exchange for past bitterness.

Circumstances will always dictate the mood of the moment and how the individual reacts to it. Now, near the end of our POW status, we were on a high note of living. We had beaten the heavy odds stacked against us and survived a race in which the principal opponent was time.

We had, for the first time, the leisure to review our experiences. We had beaten the odds that were against us – triumphed over the grim adversity in our first internment at Changi. It was a victory, too, when we crossed the South China Sea on our debilitating journey on the old *England Maru*, when we had wondered with apprehension if we could stay upright for another year. Later, as our health deteriorated, we had looked only months ahead. We had seen our beri beri; our dysentery and the other ailments of malnutrition and overwork take their toll. We had watched helpless as comrades fell before these maladies and before Japanese cruelty. We had worried when our time would come. As the calendar and clock worked their relentless and unforgiving movement, we had watched the days and the hours; the minutes and seconds. We began to invest our ambitions for survival in these fractional terms as the daily death toll mounted in the hell of Kinkasaki. By this time we had become melancholy Zombies, seeking only survival for the moment. And meanwhile our overlords, the servants of Japan and its emperor, had showed no pity or mercy and sapped even our will and our pride.

Here we had come at last, the survivors. We, the lucky ones, by the grace of God. Most of us had been taught the Christian duty of forgiveness. I found (and find) it hard to forgive and can never forget.

The Japanese, in the event, showed no sign of concern for the missing Tashi. They might even have been aware of his departure the night before.

We ate our breakfast of boiled rice and swigged the accompanying lukewarm water and went on parade for the last time in the jungle camp. Each of us was allotted a bundle of stores and we limped and stumbled back down that overhung rocky path. Some of us this time carried a different burden; they carried the weak and infirm on their own backs. But we gritted our teeth! This time it was the first step on the long journey home and we did our best to shut out the pain of the journey. There was no singing of '*Colonel Bogey*' or '*Tipperary*' or any other soldiers' song. But even the capacity to express our joy had been drained by the horrors of the last 1300 odd days. But we were happy! It was that inner, quite happiness that kept us going on as we stumbled and tottered.

We must have seemed to be in a sorry state to the people of Shinten, so gaunt and haggard had we become. There was a degree of pity on the faces that stared at us from beneath the lamp-shade-style straw hats they wore. There was no energetic waving of the 'fried-egg' flag of Japan either. We had been liberated by our victorious troops, or would be soon, and so would they. At last there had appeared a sense of kindred spirit. We boarded the train that awaited us and our journey began with no time lost. Half an hour later we arrived at another camp on the outskirts of Taihoku.

Here we settled to await the arrival of our liberators, whoever they might be and, better still, we settled with a greatly increased ration of rice than we had received during the past three years or more. But even that was not the end, since we also began to receive small luxuries like salt and lumps of solid sugar with which we stuffed ourselves. That was unfortunate since our poverty-stricken insides could not cope and we suffered punishing diarrhoea. At last, it appeared that the Japanese were softening towards us; possibly with the thought that humane acts now would be in their favour when the day of reckoning came.

Near the end of August, some huge US transport planes arrived overhead and dropped large metal containers, filled with food, for us. Their act of kindness had terrible consequences, since with it came disaster. The planes had come in too low and the parachutes attached to the containers failed to open in time to slow their descent. Those of us who were fit enough were outside waving to the aircrews who could be seen plainly by us as they stood in the open sides of the planes. They were pushing out loads of food and waving back at us as they did so. Then chaos reigned as the 'Manna from Heaven' plummeted down among us and thudded into the ground at our feet. Confusion ensued and momentary terror as men were hit and injured and some civilians who were outside the camp were injured.

I was lucky that day. Two heavy metal barrels, clamped together, missed me by inches as I darted here and there in alarm, like everyone else, to escape them. When they struck the ground the heavy shock wave, caused by their impact, was so powerful that I was lifted several feet into the air and deposited – along with accompanying lumps of turf and stones – in an undignified, but still breathing, heap on the ground some distance away. My heart pounded in fright within my protruding rib cage!

Confusion was everywhere now and spontaneous howls of terror and pain abounded. Outside the compound, civilians too, men women and children, scattered in all directions as the planes continued to drop the 'goodies' to us apparently unaware of the carnage on the ground below. Amidst this scene, some of our signal corps men were doing their best to convey to the aircrew that all was not well. After some time, the message was conveyed to the pilots who ceased the drop of death and mutilation.

There was relief now as we watched the planes speed off into the distance and time to tend to the maimed and wounded in our midst. A fair number of our men were injured with varying degrees of severity. (We had no way of knowing how badly the civilians outside the camp had fared.) Worse followed. We discovered that some people were killed, including three POWs. It is true, indeed, that 'Man cannot live by bread alone.'

How bizarre, unpredictable and dreadful Fate can be. Everyone was running furiously to escape the much-needed food that was falling from the skies. These three prisoners had escaped, at last, from their hell on Taiwan and the relentless cruelty of their captors, only to be killed by the first act of generosity they had experienced in more than three years and this from the very people who would lead them to freedom. Bloody hell! Bloody, bloody hell!

Once more I had the feeling that I had received the favour of Divine intervention. I was still alive! Some more of my comrades were not. I said a silent prayer for those fallen comrades and a prayer of thanks for myself. The quicker I was away from this cursed island of Formosa the better, I thought. My luck had to run out, sooner or later.

Only a couple of days passed before a US Marine officer and about six of his men arrived at the camp and, with little ado, told us to be ready to leave as quickly as possible. We were being transported right away. Ten minutes later we were all on parade, carrying our few belongings and carrying some of our mates who were unable to walk. We boarded a waiting train a short distance from the camp. Our liberators had come at last! The engine blew three long blasts on the whistle, as if to salute the start of our freedom, and began to gather speed on the next step of the long way home.

'Wonderful! Bloody wonderful!' I thought, as I gazed at the glum and forlorn Japanese soldiers who lined the track. They had lately been ejected from the train by a handful of US Marines in order to accommodate us. I felt proud of these soldiers who had chanced their luck in removing all those armed Japanese from the train and who had prevailed. A sense of manliness stirred in me once more. That sense, which had been absent for so long was returning. I was emerging from the region of the Zombies. I gazed at a smartly dressed young marine who stood by the carriage window, grasping his automatic rifle at the ready and prepared to die for me if necessary.

At this moment, too, I reflected on the vows that we had made during our harsh confinement, that one day we would crucify those who had crucified us. Here we were, looking at them now, the soldiers of Dai Nippon, without so much as a derogatory remark or jeer. The venom stored within me was gone, completely nullified by the blissful tranquillity, which accompanied our freedom. I was free; I had no need now for retribution. I had defeated them by being alive.

*　　*　　*

Good-bye Taihoku! Good-bye to the bloody jungle camp! Good-bye effin' Kinkasaki and the copper-mine! Thank you My Lord and My Lady! (And any others who had a hand in my survival – including, this time, the Shinto chap!).

126

Dempsey and Taffy sat beside me and we shared a quiet smile of gladness. It felt so good to be free men. Taffy was grasping Tashi's bamboo and his smile grew broader as he brandished it ferociously above his head. He frightened the young marine as he performed his Tarzan Jungle cry with newfound gusto. Just one more time! Looking out of the window I saw a shadow of fright cross the faces of the couple of Japanese soldiers who still stood by the side of the tracks. It had been a memorable end to a memorable day. Just one more small victory for us to have the last laugh. And how good it was to laugh again!

Tojo San

Ah never thocht ah'd live tae see
The day ah'd look him in the ee.
Auld Nick, ah mean – the deil hisel';
Afore ah'd even been tae hell.

Wi' horns, an' forkit tongue, an' tail;
A sicht tae see, an' make ye quail
Wi' fricht, an' shake wi' mortal fear;
His blidshot een at me did leer.

Him squattin' there wi' cloven hoof,
An' fearsome fangs in cruel mooth,
Ah tried – but couldnae bliddy run.
Mah legs were petrified, ah fun'.

So there, in splutterin' carbide licht,
In nee pan nee, ah froze wi' fricht,
As grotesque ghouls around did flit,
In Kinkasaki's hellish pit.

'Twas Lampo, Goldie, Fryin' Pan,*
An' Patchie, a' rolled intae wan.
The Great Arch Hancho, doon the mine;
Auld Tojo, san – the bliddy swine.

Noo, hirplin' near wi' evil stealth,
Ah wis concerned aboot mah health,
As bloodstained trident poised, he boasted,
'See you, Mac . . . you'll soon be roasted.'

So there ah wis – the end wis nigh:
Ah said mah prayers, prepared tae die,
As he'rt abeatin' like a drum,
Ah waited for the end tae come.

Ah shut mah een – ah'd soon be deid;
Ah said the 'hale Apostles creed,
An' hoped the Lord wid hear mah prayer,

An' stiffen Tojo, oan the flair.
An' stiffen him, he did – the Lord,
Wi' fiery cross, and bloody sword.
An' Tojo, let oot sich a scream,
It woke me up . . . 'twas but a dream.

---

* Lampo, Goldie, Frying Pan, and Patchie, were *hanchos* (overseers) in the copper mine.

7

Blighty Bound

It might be thought that, after the hardships of the past three years we should have been shouting abuse at the Japanese soldiers who had lined the railway tracks and should have been celebrating with excitement. It was not that way for us just then. We had little strength left in our malnourished bodies and minds for such rejoicing. But we had a glow of quiet happiness which wrapped itself around us now with the comforting knowledge that the gutter, in which we had shed our silent tears, had gone from us forever. This felt like a more fitting exultation and more dignified as I gave thanks for a deliverance from evil. It was right to remember the dead that we left behind.

There would come a time for singing but this was not that time.

The antiquated engine, with its taxing load of packed carriages, click-clacked onwards, speeding through Taihoku, and a number of villages and hamlets. All showed the scars left by the continual bombing by US B24s and B29s. Heaps of rubble lay everywhere and signs of the devastation stretched as far as the eye could see.

These poor people had suffered too but I could feel no compassion for them, even as I met the lack-lustre eyes of citizens and villagers staring back at me in melancholy bewilderment. My sympathy was reserved for my fallen comrades. They had surely been murdered by the Japanese by starvation and fiendish abuse. It was for them that I mourned and grieved.

In my mind was a terrible montage of their sufferings in the claustrophobic and suffocating furnaces of the 'holes' in which they had worked. I saw their struggles to meet quotas that could not be met and their subsequent knowledge of the impending encounter with the *Hancho*'s hammer. In my mind I could see proud heads drooping in shame and despair. I could identify with their suffering because I had shared it. Terrible memories swirled around in my head. I could see my own skinny body clinging to compressed air-pipes above my head as the repulsive Frying Pan laid bare the scant flesh on my legs and posterior. And so I kept my compassion for my own comrades in the bloodstained abyss we had inhabited.

At last, as I thought of these things, I felt a wetness affect my eyes. I thought of my comrades, who paid the price of patriotism and who were denied even Christian burial. One shilling! Cheap at the bloody price. No cheap crocodile tears were ever as wet as the tears that I felt now.

My morbid thoughts were brought to an abrupt end as the train juddered to a halt at the dockside in Keelung. Here were more American soldiers who lost no time in transferring us to two destroyers that waited there. The destroyers then picked their way through the sunken ships that lay in the harbour while the well armed and friendly US Marines watched over us.

Further out in the bay we were transferred again to an awaiting American aircraft carrier. After getting into a large lifeboat, which carried us from ship to ship, I was put aboard the carrier, transferred literally hand-to-hand from one US serviceman to another on board the huge warship.

Once aboard, we were stripped of our ragged clothing and given clean, denim, sailor's trousers, a white vest and a 'pork-pie' sailor's hat. Our old clothes were contemptuously thrown overboard into the turbulent water. We were shaved of all of our bodily hair, made to shower with strong carbolic soap and finally sprayed with some kind of disinfectant. This last task was carried out by crewmen dressed in long, protective clothing with a head covering, like visitors from another planet.

Best of all, we were given our first real meal for three and a half years. It was wonderful, fit for a king (even George VI). We had meat and veg followed by as much ice-cream and fruit as we could eat and all washed down with a bottle of beer and accompanied by a packet of US Cigarettes for each man. All of the things we had dreamed of for so long and which had seemed as utterly unattainable as the bloody moon. It was so wonderful. Our hosts treated us like brothers and waited upon us hand and foot. To complete a perfect day there was a comfortable, clean bed with white sheets and warm blankets.

It felt like the Ritz. After our years of rice and lukewarm water, all this really felt like VIP treatment. My coolie days were surely over. I was the equal of all in the land with the attention and even adulation I was receiving on this mighty warship of Uncle Sam's.

If captivity had been hell, the next few days were heaven on that magnificent, floating hotel. Most marked of all its pleasures was the absence of the ready rifle butt or blows from our hosts. We could have been accused of greed, perhaps even gluttony, but in the circumstances our hosts readily forgave us our sins.

After the ship berthed in the Philipinnes and we had been given a month of intensive and concerned medical attention from our American friends, we were confronted by a choice. We could either go home via Australia by plane or by ship via the United States.

John Dempsey Kane decided upon the Australian route while Taffy and I chose the American one. A few days later, we said our good-byes to Dempsey and boarded the Marine Shark, a brand-new Liberty ship. After the weeks of kindness and care from the Americans this was, indeed, icing on the cake.

Taffy and I strode the decks of this new ship, sharing our slight worry for Dempsey. The Dakota, the plane in which he would travel, had a reputation of being accident prone. Little did we know that the Liberty ships had just as bad a record for breaking up in bad weather, having been welded, as opposed to the more usual riveting of their plates. Finding out did not help our peace of mind. When we sailed from Manila next morning, I prayed for a safe passage home. I need hardly have bothered since a major storm broke out with gale-force winds and turbulent seas pounding the plates of the ship's hull which, in my fevered imagination, were about to break assunder at any moment. I wished with all my heart that we had gone on the Dakota with John Kane. Perhaps my Heavenly Benefactors had tired of giving me handouts and had decided to leave me to my own devices.

The next six days for the Marine Shark were a good test for her welded plates, as the mighty Pacific pounded them ferociously. She rolled from port to starboard and back while all aboard were thrown around with much cursing and swearing – and not a little praying! The bows would dig deep into the gigantic waves lifting the stern and screws clear of the water with much juddering. My thoughts remained fixed upon what I had heard of these lovely ships breaking up.

The weather calmed (and so did I, but more slowly) and the hull was still intact. My palpitating heart gave three cheers for the skill of the skipper. We eventually arrived in America after sailing under the Golden Gate bridge at San Francisco and tied up at one of the quays. As we trooped down the gangway, a GI band blared forth with a jaunty jazzy version of 'I belong to Glasgow' and then 'Land of Hope and Glory' with the same style. I felt an uncontrollable emotion within me. Tears welled up again in my eyes. I was really back home among my 'Ain Folk,' no matter that they were Yanks, just my far-flung kith and kin. I had some pride again.

May God Bless America! I saluted the generous and caring people who thronged the dockside cheering and applauding as we passed on our way to waiting Army trucks. Their acknowledgement of us as human beings did as much to speed our recovery as the dozens of vitamin tablets that we were given each day to build us up. The recognition by the people of this mighty nation was a powerful morale booster and I felt my shoulders begin to square up once more. I felt like a man again and could now look to the future when, such a short time ago I had none.

The trucks pulled away from the docks and drove along the river. We passed the island of Alcatraz and, further up river, stopped at a military depot where we were fully kitted out. A train was waiting which took us to Seattle. In that north western city we dallied for four days enjoying the hospitality of the local people and those from nearby Tacoma. All were friendly and wonderful and I would never forget them.

After four days, we boarded another train with comfortable Pullman carriages and splendid heating, which kept out the November chill. We crossed into Canada and I marvelled at the vast, open, snow-covered plains and the great mountains in the far distance.

The Canadian people were generous also, offering gifts and sympathy on the way. Four and a half days later, we boarded the *Queen Mary* at New York. We had reached the last lap of our memorable journey home. We were beginning to feel an intense longing for home now and our arrival on the great ship, this time a British one, was an important stage in our homecoming.

We reflected that our survival had been due in no small part to British Sergeants, Sergeant-Majors and especially cooks. They had toughened us up with square bashing and 'bullshit' while the cooks had weighed in with gruelly porridge and burnt, boiled eggs. The cooks had followed up with their unique secret recipe for Spotted Dick or Plum Duff that could sink battleships. Knowing that nothing else was on offer the squaddie would eat, sometimes even without complaint. After these combined efforts the British Soldier was better equipped for survival than most others.

The Messing Officer on the Queen Mary, must have had a plan in mind when he created the menu. From the excesses of the food in Canada and the USA we were plunged immediately back to the reality of Cooking, Army Style. We were served lentil Soup with particles of hambone dispersed through it. An old Scottish favourite followed as we received 'tatties and mince' with a dollop of water-logged cabbage. But the highlight of the evening had yet to come – Spotted Dick! and just as we remembered it. Just to show that I could enter into the spirit, I took up the challenge offered – but failed. I never found the currant!

Friday the 13th is not normally regarded as a propitious sailing date for sailors (who are usually regarded as being highly superstitious) The Captain of the *Queen Mary*, however, was in considerate mood and assumed that we all wanted to be back home as quickly as possible. His gigantic charge, therefore slipped her moorings on 13 November, 1945, and slid smoothly from the dockside, aided by a few New York tugs. She was soon headed for the Atlantic Ocean.

Now we would soon be home again and Taffy and I watched as the tall buildings of the Manhattan skyline faded into the distance and were soon lost from view. We had followed a long, rock-strewn path since leaving Lanark and now we were going home aboard this mighty Clyde-built liner. 'Going home in style, and deservedly so', I told myself, as the *Queen* ploughed through the choppy sea with contempt. This was no frail Liberty ship. The stout metal from the steel works of Lanarkshire tore the waves apart and pulverized them.

'Built at John Brown's, Clydebank' a well-polished brass plate announced to the world. As Taffy and I stood looking at it and reading it aloud, I could not help but feel that I had a share in it.

Taffy was still a little at odds with himself from the beating he had received at the Changi beach burial party. He was becoming quite animated at the prospect of seeing Maggie again and 'little Taffy', as he called him. He was still confused at times and smiling or morose at others. I was very concerned for him in the immediate future. How would he cope if the meeting with the girl he had once demeaned on a troop train proved unproductive. He had become adamant that she would be waiting for him.

So I would listen to his muted whispers, 'Maggie' and 'Little Taffy Mcbloody Tavish', as he would smile and call Maggie's bairn and his bairn too. And I would watch his eyes shine when he mentioned them. I hoped for the best. Some of the soldiers aboard the *Queen Mary* had been kept alive simply by the prospect of someday returning to their homes and families. As it turned out, some of them, now that they were free, had received 'Dear John' letters from wives or sweethearts. I had seen already the distress and grief that such an event could have. It was a truly crucifying home-coming. I wondered, again, at the seeming lack of compassion from 'Jock Tamson' for his wounded 'bairns'.

With all this misery and unhappiness around me, I was seriously concerned as to how it would affect Taffy if he, too, received the cold shoulder. I broached the subject, trying to prepare him. I warned him of the possibility that she might have found someone else, might even be married. He was adamant. Lanark it was and Maggie and Taffy would be waiting for him. Wales and his parents could wait until later, when he would take Maggie and Taffy to see them. Maggie was his priority and nothing was going to change his mind. That was that. I had done what I could and had no more to offer.

Four days on the *Queen Mary* passed and the south coast of England now hove into sight. We docked at Southampton and had reached British soil at last.

How good it was to feel the earth of home underfoot again. I had avoided 'Boothill,' as we had called the makeshift cemetery at Kinkasaki. We went to a clearance camp nearby and were subjected to medical examinations of various kinds. At last, after another stodgy army meal, trucks took us to the railway stations en route for home.

Euston was the terminal for Glasgow and Lanarkshire and we were soon on our way home. Another moment we had dreamed of had arrived and there was an air of quiet contentment in our compartment of the carriage. There was none of the singing or rough banter which is characteristic of soldiers in transit, just peaceful contemplation of the joyful reunions that awaited us. We were winners against the odds and alive to tell the tale, while others had fallen by the wayside. Each withdrew to the seclusion of his own thoughts.

Lanark Station arrived and I got off with Taffy. It was not my home town but if things did not go well between him and Maggie then I would be around to take him home with me until he could sort himself out. He strode purposefully to the 'foot o' the toon' where Maggie lived, with a confident smile upon his rugged face. I hoped he would still be smiling when Maggie opened the door. I crossed my fingers and hoped that the smile he was wearing was a good omen.

It was afternoon and the town was quiet. There were few locals to abuse us as we made our way down the High Street in the direction of her house. He was in a joyously excited state; confidence that she would be there flowed from him. He muttered their names over and over as he shouldered his heavy kitbag and strode eagerly forward.

As we neared the corner leading to her house I returned to prayer. 'Please, God, don't let this happen to my mate'. We turned the corner and one house was bedecked with balloons, bunting and assorted flags.

Prayers are answered! Above the door of the house was the most wonderful message I could have seen. 'Welcome home, Taffy!' As both of us stood there, gaping at the wonderful words, the door opened and Maggie McTavish stood there. She opened her arms wide to him.

My burly mate let his kitbag slide to the ground and, holding out his arms, walked towards her. They embraced. Taffy repeated, as if he had learnt them by heart the words he had said over and over during the years since his beating on the beach. 'Maggie, Maggie McTavish, my Maggie.' Then a little lad of about four or five years appeared at the door. Taffy glanced at Maggie with an open question. She nodded. It was his son! Taffy McTavish Morgan.

More joy, then, more smiles! He lifted the child and kissed and admired him but hardly had he done so than another child appeared and this time a little girl. She was about a year younger than the little boy with black hair and blue eyes and she walked to Maggie saying, 'Mammy!'

Taffy was transformed now as he looked, with a look of hurt and accusation, at her and then at Maggie. Just as I wished to be a hundred miles away, Maggie wagged a finger at the glowering Taffy.

'Bronwyn, I called her, after your mother, you daft Welsh bugger. This is your daughter. Have you forgotten that we went to Lanark Loch the night before you went away? And drunk as a puggy you were! and widnae take no for an answer.' Taffy relaxed again and smiled. He lifted the child and held both her and Maggie close. There were tears in Maggie's eyes, a by-product of long years of lost living which had been found again. Tears of happiness.

I was surplus to requirements now, with this intense scene of personal emotion going on around me. Certainly Taffy did not need me, now that he had Maggie as his companion. Time to be off. I said my goodbyes, wishing them luck and happiness and shouldered my kitbag, thinking now of my own homecoming and my own loved ones.

I paused, momentarily, at the old Kirk at the 'foot o' the toon' where mighty William Wallace stood in his niche. He stood massive and fearsome, grasping his huge sword and, as I looked at him, I wondered how he would have fared against the relentless Japanese advance during the Malayan Campaign. Would his mighty claymore, encrusted with the blood of valiant Englishmen, have been of any use?

'Nae chance, Willie!' I decided. 'Yamashita would have sent you hame tae'. I reflected that the achievements of both Wallace and Yamashita were now part of the unchanging past. But both would be written about by historians who could adapt or change their deeds at will. They would become as the writers portrayed them to be. And I too! The pen is mightier than the bloody sword.

I left Sir William to sulk at my lack of enthusiasm. He might not be pleased either at the lack of respect shown by the Lanark pigeons. Then I rounded the corner to await the bus that would finally take me home.

As I stood, I looked at the Clydesdale Hotel nearby and a flood of memories came back. I thought of 1939 when we still had our horses and swords, our pants, puttees and spurts and when the discipline we faced in those early months of the war was relatively relaxed. On one winter morning I had been part of a duty squad, marching past the hotel. I saw the strange sight of our regimental trumpeter, standing at the close mouth,★ sounding reveille while clad only in thick semmit(vest) and a pair of long Johns which he held up with his free left hand. This was, of course, an affront to King's Regulations which states with emphasis

> Long-legged woollen underwear must not be displayed while sounding reveille.

Those were early days and no one had seemed to mind about the odd indiscretion. We were young and more like a large family. But possibly our laxity with regard to the King's regulations had contributed to our being named 'Fireside Sodjers'. That, anyway combined with our over-long stay at Lanark.

The Number 240 bus squeaked to a halt and I climbed aboard and watched the familiar Lanarkshire scenery pass by as it sped me onwards to Home, Sweet Home.

★   ★   ★

From now on I would be a 'Fireside Civilian' and hug the hearth forever. My away-days were over, my troubles behind me. I would never recoup my lost years but I would always be thankful I survived them.

★ Close mouth: a Scottish term for an entry, narrow or wide, which gives passage to a dwelling or commercial yard, the 'mouth' being the front.

For the future, I had a new yardstick. It was the certainty that nothing in it could be as bad as the past.

I had been dead at Kinkasaki and had emerged from the fires of Hell to live again. With this in mind, I give one final accolade to my Saviour,

'Aregatto, Hancho San, . . . Aregatto'

They Shall Not Be Forgotten
1941–1945

In proud and unfading memory of the Officers, NCOs and Men of th 155th (Lanarkshire Yeomanry) Field Regiment, Royal Artillery, wh gave their lives during the Malayan Campaign of 1941–42 or died in th aftermath of those valiant and meritorious battles as prisoners of war, th victims of Japanese brutality and the harsh, disease-ridden condition under which they slaved and lived.

Their shattered bodies are gone but their immortal souls live on in th hearts and minds of all who knew them and shared the dangers and priva tions of those dark years.

Lt.Colonel Murdoch A.T.D.	★Captain Coles G.R.	★Lt. Anderson M.L.
Major Wilson J.	Captain Eustace M.J.K.	★2/Lt. Ronaldson
★Captain Stewart J.H.W.	Captain Forster A.R.	2/Lt. Wynne J.G.
★A/Sgt. Anderson W.G.	★Gnr. Andrews E.G.	★Bdr. Annis F.A.
★L/Bdr. Askew H.	★Gnr. Bailey H.A.	★L/Sgt. Barnes E.F.
★Gnr. Barnes E.	★BQMS Bartlett A.C.	Bdr. Bennet G.J.E.
WO2 Billings F.J.	★Bdr. Black J.	★L/Bdr. Blair W.V.
★Gnr. Brown G.M.	★Gnr. Buchanan R.	★Gnr. Burns H
★Gnr. Byers W.J.J.	★Gnr. Cadell D.	★Gnr. Callan R.
★L/Bdr. Calland W.	★Gnr. Campbell R.	Gnr. Carroll J.

Bdr. Cavers A.S.I.	*Gnr. Christie A.H.	*Gnr. Collins F.
Gnr. Cowan J.	*Gnr. Crawford T.	*Gnr Cunningham W.
L/Bdr. Cuthbertson S.	*Gnr. Daly W.	*Gnr. Dalziel W.R.
Bdr. Donnelly T.F.	*Gnr. Douglas J.W.	Bdr. Edel B.
Gnr. Emery T.A.	Gnr. Edgar T.	*Gnr. Eldhouse E.
L/Bdr. Ellerby G.	*Bdr. Evans J.H.	*L/Bdr. Farmer J.C.
Bdr. Flint G.V.	Bdr. Gaillard R.P.	*Gnr. Glendinning G.R.
Gnr. Gordon G.	*Gnr. Gordon T.	*L/Bdr. Graham J.
Gnr. Graham G.M.	*Gnr. Grieg J.	*Gnr. Grierson W.J.
Gnr. Gunn A.	*L/Sgt. Halifax J.	Gnr. Hall M.W.
Gnr. Herker H.	*Bdr. Henderson S.	*Gnr. Hendry J.
Bdr. Hiddleston D.M.	*Gnr. Hoskins F.	*Gnr. James J.W.
Gnr. Johnson E.	*Gnr. Johnston W.J.	L/Sgt. Keen O.J.
L/Bdr. Kelly J.M.	*Gnr. Laing D.A.K.L.	*Gnr. Lindley F.S.
Gnr. Little D.G.	*Gnr. Logan R.	*Gnr. Lovage G.
Gnr. Lowther M.B.	*Gnr. McCallum D.	Gnr. McDonald J.
Gnr. McKenna J.	*Gnr. McLean A.	*Gnr. Medlock A.
Gnr. Moore T.D.	*Gnr. Padgett E.	*S/Sgt. Parker J.J.
Gnr. Patterson J.M.	*Bdr. Pennington R.C.	*L/Bdr. Perman G.
Gnr. Pickles S.	*Gnr. Powell J.	Gnr. Quartier A.G.
Gnr. Ramsay H.S.	*Gnr. Rose E.B.	*Gnr. Scott I.
Gnr. Scott J.	*Gnr. Schun C.W.A.	*Bdr. Sinclair T.A.B.
Gnr. Smith H.C.	*Bdr. Speed H.	*Gnr. Spurrier A.W.
Gnr. Steward E.	*Gnr. Stone S.D.G.	*Gnr. Street A.C.
Gnr. Sweeney D.	*L/Bdr. Tadman T.W.	Gnr. Taylor G.
Gnr. Thompson R.	*Gnr. Topping J.F.	*Gnr. Tuck S.H.
Gnr. Vanstone R.H.	*Gnr. Vere A.	*Gnr. Wain F.
Gnr. Warnock H.	*Gnr. Webster E.	L/Bdr. Winslow W.

*Died as prisoners of war in Japanese hands